Iron Age Hillfort Defences and the Tactics of Sling Warfare

Peter Robertson

Archaeopress Archaeology

Archaeopress Publishing Ltd
Gordon House
276 Banbury Road
Oxford OX2 7ED

www.archaeopress.com

ISBN 978 1 78491 410 3
ISBN 978 1 78491 411 0 (e-Pdf)

© Archaeopress and P Robertson 2016

Printed and bound in Great Britain by
Marston Book Services Ltd, Oxfordshire

All rights reserved. No part of this book may be reproduced, stored in retrieval system, or transmitted, in any form or by any means, electronic, mechanical, photocopying or otherwise, without the prior written permission of the copyright owners.

This book is available direct from Archaeopress or from our website www.archaeopress.com

Contents

Abstract viii

Preface ix

Acknowledgements x

Chapter 1: Introduction 1

Chapter 2: Iron Age Hillfort Defences 4
   Distinguishing Hillforts and Hillfort Defences 4
   Hillfort Investigations 5
   Development of Hillforts during the Iron Age 6
      General Pattern of Hillfort Development 6
      Development of the Defences 8
         Variations 9
      Entrances 10
         Variations 14
         Guard Chambers 14
         Bridges and Towers 16
         Exposure of Unshielded Side 16
         Entrances without Gates 16
   Hod Hill 16
   The Function of Hillfort Defences 18
   Warfare at Hillforts 24

Chapter 3: The Sling and Sling Warfare 26
   Construction and Operation of Slings 26
      Shot 26
   Archaeological Evidence 27
      Sling-stones 27
      Slings 29
      Skeletal Trauma 29
   Uses of Slings 29
   Range of Slings 30
   Effect of Sling Hits 31
   Accuracy 34
   Tactics of Sling Warfare 34

Chapter 4: Background to the Experiment ... 35

Chapter 5: The Experiment ... 39
Approach ... 39
Practical Issues ... 39
Availability and Skills of Participants ... 39
Sling-stones ... 40
Weather ... 40
Phased Approach ... 40
Experiment Method ... 41
Site ... 41
Survey ... 41
Experimental Conditions and Variables ... 43
Excluded Conditions ... 45
Measurements ... 46
Repeated Measures Design ... 47
Participants ... 47
Experience of Slingers ... 48
Casting Style ... 48
Equipment ... 48
Slings ... 48
Sling-stones ... 49
Target ... 51
Signals and Notices ... 52
Procedure ... 52
Safety and Ethics ... 53
Results ... 53
Qualitative Results and Observations ... 54
Approximate Accuracy and Range ... 54
Downhill and Uphill Slinging ... 54
Slinging from Sloping Stances ... 54
Slinging Styles ... 55
Effectiveness of Hits ... 56
Accuracy and Timing Results ... 56
Key to Abbreviations and Graphs of Results ... 56
Summary Statistics ... 57
Attack Versus Defence ... 59
Univallate Versus Bivallate ... 59
Distance to Target ... 60
Correlations ... 60
Analysis of Variance ... 62
Effective Range ... 64
Time Required to Assault the Defences ... 64

    Tactical Analysis 65
        Scenario 1: Direct Assault by Small Group of Attackers 65
            Probability of Being Hit during an Assault.. 68
            Other Factors 70
        Scenario 2: Barrage from the Edge of the Defences............................... 70
            Defensive Reinforcements 72
            Slinging Effectiveness 73
        Scenario 3: Two-Stage Assault and Defence of Bivallate Defences 74
        Assaults on Entrances 75
        Surprise or Diversionary Tactics 76

Chapter 6: Discussion 77
    Functions of Hillforts and Hillfort Defences 77
        Defensive Features and Characteristics.. 77
        Evidence of Other Functions 79
        Authors' Perspectives and Consensus 81
    The Experiment and Analysis 81
        Interpreting the Data 81
        Representativeness of the Iron Age 83
    Further Tactical Considerations 84
        The Nature of Iron Age Warfare 86

Chapter 7: Conclusions 88

Appendix A: Procedure Exhibits and Experiment Equipment............................ 89
    Participant Instructions – Introduction 90
    Safety and Environment Briefing to Participants....................................... 91
    Participant Slinging Instructions 92
    Data Record Sheet 93
    Advanced Notice – At Site Entrances 94
    Warning Notice 95
    Participant Details Record (1).. 96
    Participant Details Record (2).. 97
    Emergency Instructions 98
    Safety Analysis and Plan 99
        Introduction 99
        Overview of the experiment 99
        Risk Analysis 99
        Safety Procedures 100
        Review 101
        Exhibits... 101
    Ethics Analysis and Plan 102
        Introduction 102
        Overview of the experiment 102

Ethical Factors Influencing the Experimental Procedures 103
Health and Safety risks to participants and others 103
Embarrassments to participants 104
Deception of participants.. 104
Motivation of participants 104
Handling participants' details... 104
Feedback and acknowledgements to participants................................ 104
Exclusion of data 105
Damage to environment 105
Independent Review 105
Documentation 105
Equipment.. 105

Appendix B: Experiment Results and Data Analyses............................ 108
Participant Data... 108
Raw Slinging Data.. 108
Analyses of Variance 111
Descriptive Statistics 113
Same on The Ground 114
Relative to Defenders 115
Details of Results 116
Time of Assault... 116
Accuracy and Slinging Time 116
Effective Range... 116
Tactical Analyses.. 116

Bibliography 122

List of Figures

Figure 1. Distribution of Larger Hillforts in Southern Britain. 2
Figure 2. Hoard of 22260 Sling-stones at Maiden Castle 6
Figure 3. Concentration of Hillfort Use in Middle and Later Iron Age 7
Figure 4. Timber Box Rampart Constructions 8
Figure 5. Glacis-style Rampart. 9
Figure 6. Stone Defences at Tre'r Ceiri 10
Figure 7. *Chevaux-de-Frise* at Dun Aengus, Co. Galway 11
Figure 8. Milber Down Multiple Enclosure Hillfort 11
Figure 9. Three In-Turned Entrances 12
Figure 10. Remains of Stone-Wall Entrance Passage at Maiden Castle, Swaledale 13
Figure 11. Five Developed Entrances 14
Figure 12. Maiden Castle, Dorset, Showing Multivallate Defences and the Western Entrance 15
Figure 13. Rampart Kink Suggesting Blocked Entrance at Cadbury, Devon 15
Figure 14. Aerial Photograph of Hod Hill from the East 17
Figure 15. Geophysical Survey of Hod Hill Interior 18
Figure 16. Development of Hod Hill Defences 19
Figure 17. Section of Northern Defences of Hod Hill 20
Figure 18. Enclosed Hilltop above Ramparts at Hambledon Hill. 21
Figure 19. The Orientation of 75 Hillfort Entrances in Southern England 22
Figure 20. Reproduction Plaited Sling 26
Figure 21. Roman Biconical Shot 27
Figure 22. Hoard of Sling-stones near Eastern Entrance of Maiden Castle 27
Figure 23. Clay Shot from Danebury 28
Figure 24. Leather Panels from Medieval York 29
Figure 25. Sling-Stone Trajectories Plotted against Hillfort Profiles 30
Figure 26. Peruvian Slinger in Trials Reported by Brown, Vega and Craig 31
Figure 27. Roman Auxiliary Slinger on Trajan's Column 32
Figure 28. High Dump Glacis Rampart at Hambledon Hill. 36
Figure 29. Sling-stone Trajectories Plotted against the Northern Defences of Hod Hill 37
Figure 30. Location Map for Hod Hill 42
Figure 31. Aerial View of Hod Hill from the West; Experiment Site is Bottom-Left 43
Figure 32. Inner Rampart and Ditch of Hod Hill, Seen from Outer Rampart 44
Figure 33. Plan of North-West Section of Hod Hill, Showing Slinging Lines 45

Figure 34. Univallate Profile and Slinging Positions 46
Figure 35. Bivallate Profile and Slinging Positions 46
Figure 36. Repeated Measures Experimental Design 47
Figure 37. Andean Sling 48
Figure 38. Modern Sling Similar to One Used in the Experiment 49
Figure 39. Staff Sling 49
Figure 40. Selection of Sling-stones 50
Figure 41. Comparison of Air-Dried Clay (Bottom Row) and Other Types of Shot 50
Figure 42. Target 51
Figure 43. Target on Inner Face of Outer Rampart, Guyed Upright 52
Figure 44. Overall Slinging Results by Participant 53
Figure 45. Sling-stone Holes in Medium-Density Target 55
Figure 46. Table of Abbreviations Used in Results Charts 56
Figure 47. Legend for Results Charts 57
Figure 48. Average Hit Rates by Condition 57
Figure 49. Overall Hits by Position, All Participants 58
Figure 50. Time for Six Casts, by Participant and Position 58
Figure 51. Univallate Hit Rates, All Participants 59
Figure 52. Bivallate Hit Rates, All Participants 60
Figure 53. Defending Hit Rates, Participant 1-1D 61
Figure 54. Attacking Hit Rates, Participant 1-1D 61
Figure 55. Probability of Hit on Inner Target versus Distance, All Participants 62
Figure 56. Probability of Total Hits versus Distance, All Participants 62
Figure 57. Probability of Total Hits versus Distance, Participant 1-1D 63
Figure 58. Statistical Significance Summary from ANOVA 64
Figure 59. Timing and Attacking Shots for Scenario 1 66
Figure 60. Individual Hits for Scenario 1 66
Figure 61. Defensive Advantage, Shown as Ratio and Difference in Hits per Man, for Scenario 1 67
Figure 62. Hits per Individual in Grouped Attack and Defence 67
Figure 63. Probability of Attacker Reaching Hand-to-Hand Combat for Three Speed-Tactic Combinations 68
Figure 64. Probability of Attacker Reaching Hand-to-Hand Combat Distance for Three Speed-Tactic Combinations, Including Effect of Attacking Shots 69
Figure 65. Probability of Attacker Reaching Hand-to-Hand Combat for Selected Slinging Effectiveness Values 69
Figure 66. Results of Barrages 71

Figure 67. Numbers of Attackers or Defenders Left Standing for 24 Rounds of Slinging, for Three Levels of Effectiveness 72

Figure 68. Phase 3b Entrance at Crickley Hill.. 76

Figure 69. Southern Defences of Maiden Castle, Swaledale 78

Figure 70. The Target Represented a Group of Opponents 106

Figure 71. Clay Shot Broken by Impact on Target 106

Figure 72. Hole in Net Caused by Sling-stone... 107

Figure 73. Sling-stone Having Penetrated Cardboard and Foam 107

Figure 74. Participant Data 108

Figure 75. Raw Data for Participants 1-6 109

Figure 76. Raw Data for Participants 1A-1D and 7... 110

Figure 77. ANOVA for 'Same on the Ground' Positions. 112

Figure 78. ANOVA for 'Relative to Defenders' Positions. 113

Figure 79. Details for Same on the Ground Analysis 114

Figure 80. Details for Relative to Defenders Analysis 115

Figure 81. Exposure Times of Attackers by Area of the Defences 116

Figure 82. Hits by Position, All Participants 117

Figure 83. Hits by Position, Participant 1-1D 118

Figure 84. Average Time for Six Casts by Position 118

Figure 85. Results of Effective Range Informal Trial 119

Figure 86. Effective Range Compared to Finney.. 119

Figure 87. Probability of Attacker or Defender Being Hit at Least Once.................... 120

Figure 88. Probability of Attacker Reaching Hand-to-Hand Distance 120

Figure 89. Effect of Reinforcing Outnumbered Defenders at Various Intervals........... 121

Abstract

The defensive function of Iron Age hillforts has been disputed, on the grounds that they are poorly suited to military purposes and because recent models of Iron Age society emphasise symbolic display, community-building and boundaries, rather than warfare. Although excavation of hillfort interiors provides evidence of varied functions, these do not explain the features of the surrounding banks and ditches: in this study, the functions of the enclosing works are argued to be distinct from the functions of the hillfort interiors.

Pebbles found in large numbers at hillforts are interpreted as sling-stones, slings having been widely used as weapons in ancient times, and several writers have suggested that Middle Iron Age modifications to hillfort defences improved their capability against attack by stoning. However, there is little information on sling performance in the context of hillforts.

An experimental examination of these issues is described. Seven slingers cast a total of 1278 stones at a target placed in 14 positions on the defences of a hillfort, representing attack and defence of a univallate rampart and of a bivallate dump rampart. The most practiced slinger had hit-rates of 29% against a man-sized target and 68% against a target representing a group of six attackers. His effective range was over 70m. Attackers scored more hits in the univallate case, and defenders in the bivallate case. Distance to target was the main predictor of hit-rate, height being advantageous only at marginal range. Observations include the need for context-specific training and that dead ground in the outer ditch was not a defensive disadvantage.

The results were used to model several tactical scenarios, including direct assaults and barrages of stones. In general the defenders had the advantage, especially in the bivallate case, the time of exposure to defensive slinging being a key factor. Speed, surprise and superior slinging effectiveness on the part of attackers could overcome the disadvantage, but the availability of reinforcements would determine the outcome in favour of the defence in the bivallate case. Other factors, including shields, parapets and entrance designs are discussed, as are methodological issues and problems of interpretation.

The study concludes that defence remains the most persuasive functional explanation for the features of the enclosing works of hillforts.

Preface

This book is derived from a Master of Research in Archaeology dissertation for the University of Winchester. Creating new knowledge through research was an objective of the work, leading to the need for some kind of archaeological field work to qualify it as research, and hence to an experimental study which made a one-person investigation practicable.

Having worked on human performance studies in a former career, I was able to apply old skills to the conduct of such an experiment, and I hope that the methodological approach is not only novel (I have found nothing similar in the literature on hillforts or slinging) but also will provide ideas for other experimental archaeologists. For this reason, the appendixes include exhibits of the documents used in the planning and conduct of the experiment and full details of the results.

Although I refer to it above as a one-person investigation, it was of course dependent upon help from others. I am very grateful to those who supported me by providing access to the site and especially to the participants who turned up there to trial their expertise as slingers.

The cover image shows a slinger on the main rampart at Hod Hill. Photographs are by the author except where specified.

Acknowledgements

This work would not have been completed without the support of numerous individuals and several organisations. I am very grateful to everyone who helped me in understanding hillforts or with the experiment, and wish to acknowledge the following help in particular.

Dr Nick Thorpe and Dr Keith Wilkinson, of the University of Winchester Archaeology department, provided encouragement and advice throughout the conduct of this investigation.

I am grateful to the National Trust and their Property Manager, Rob Rhodes, for permission to use Hod Hill. The NT Archaeologist, Dr Martin Papworth, gave much-appreciated support in arranging the access and made helpful comments on the experiment plan.

Matthew Lovering and Roy Harrison gave time and energy to assist the survey and assault time trial at Hod Hill and acted as sounding boards during the planning.

Expert slingers from *Slinging.org* provided much information and not a few opinions on all matters relating to slings, visited a few hillforts with me, and cast the majority of the stones in the experiment. I am indebted to 'David Morningstar' and especially to 'Curious Aardvark,' without whose contributions the experiment would have flopped.

I am also grateful to *Brigantia* for providing several volunteer slingers, and especially to Matthew Curl, who organised their participation as well as slinging stones himself.

The Hillfort Study Group gave me encouragement and the opportunity to debate with real experts in the field; literally in fields on several occasions. Among them I must especially thank Dr Jon Finney, whose work was part of the inspiration for this study and who also participated in the experiment, and Professor Gary Lock, who first introduced me to the debate on the function of hillforts and who provided the opportunity to excavate at Moel y Gaer.

A number of authors and institutions have been generous with permission to reproduce figures from their work; I am grateful to Grahame Austin, Ann Boddy, Ian Brown, Margaret Brown Vega, Barry Cunliffe, Philip Dixon, Jon Finney, JD Hill, Alex Johnson, Val Maxfield, Christine McDonnell, Kate Owen, Cynthia Poole, David Stewart, Sami Taha and Anthony Weir. Nathalie Barrett generously prepared the maps and plan, from open-source data; I am very grateful to her for the time and expertise she spent on this.

Finally, my wife Elizabeth was patient and supportive as always, through many hours on the hill or at the keyboard.

Chapter 1: Introduction

'THE RULES OF DEFENCE HAVE BEEN THE SAME THROUGHOUT ALL TIME, AND ARE EXTREMELY SIMPLE' (LANE FOX 1877: 501).

Hillforts are the most prominent surviving monuments from later prehistory in Britain, but over a century of investigation has not led to them being fully understood; their size, numbers and variability have produced a variety of conflicting interpretations.

This investigation examines a specific area of debate: the function of the surrounding banks, ditches and entrances that identify Iron Age sites as hillforts. The study also focusses on sling warfare, because frequent finds of sling-stones at hillforts suggest that slings were used in their defence. A number of authors, including Wheeler (1943), Collis (1975), Avery (1993a) and Finney (2006), have proposed that some hillforts were developed in the Middle Iron Age to provide improved defence against attack by slingers. Others, notably Bowden and McOmish (1987; 1989), Hill (1993; 1996) and Lock (2011), dispute this interpretation on the grounds that hillforts were unsuitable for defence, or based on contrary views about Iron Age society and warfare.

Figure 1 shows the distribution of the major sites in southern Britain. As the number of hillforts in Britain runs into some thousands and their use spanned almost a millennium, variations in their construction were inevitable, leading to some uncertainty as to which monuments should be included in the category (for example, many are not on hills). As this study is primarily concerned with hillfort defences, no Iron Age site enclosed by a substantial bank and ditch is excluded.

The debate on the defensive suitability of the enclosing works includes little tactical analysis, partly because of the lack of information concerning the performance of slings in the context of the defence of hillforts; the experimental part of the study attempts to fill these gaps.

The characteristics and development of British hillforts and more specifically of hillfort defences are summarised in Chapter 2, followed by a review of the debate on their function. A key point is that the function of the defences can be independent of the varying functions of the hillforts themselves.

The uses of slings and their capabilities as weapons are covered in Chapter 3, including evidence from classical authors and from finds at hillforts as well as experimental evidence for sling performance.

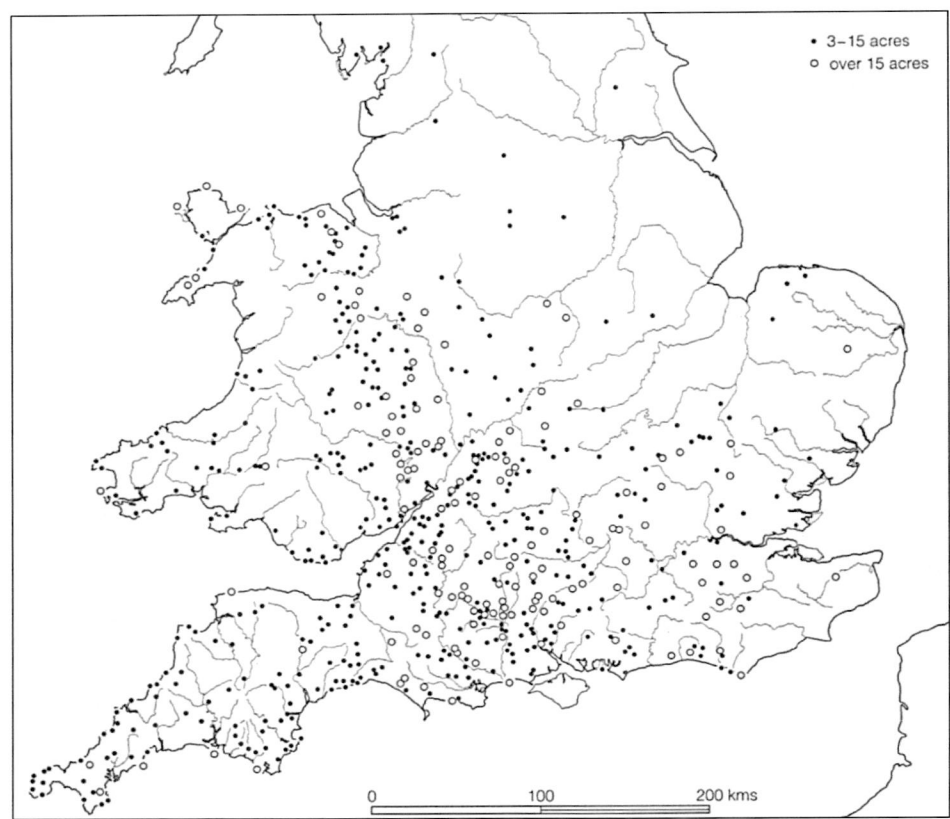

FIGURE 1. DISTRIBUTION OF LARGER HILLFORTS IN SOUTHERN BRITAIN
(FROM CUNLIFFE 2005, FIGURE 15.1, 348; BY KIND PERMISSION OF BARRY CUNLIFFE).

Chapter 4 brings the work of Michael Avery (1986; 1993a) and Jon Finney (2006) together with the foregoing material and develops the idea of an experiment to explore Avery's hypothesis that the Middle Iron Age developments of large glacis-shaped ramparts and multivallation were defensive responses to attack by stoning.

The experiment compared the performance of slingers, in both defence and attack, on hillfort ramparts roughly representative of the defences from before and after the change. Chapter 5 reports the experiment, and informal trials of range and effectiveness of slings; its major sections describe the approach, the method in detail, the principal results, and a tactical analysis modelled on the experiment data.

Chapter 6 reviews the various explanations of the presence and features of the enclosing works, followed by discussion of issues with the experiment method and with interpreting the experimental results and analyses. A summary of conclusions follows, in Chapter 7.

Two appendices include further details of the experiment equipment and procedures, and tables of results and statistical analyses.

The chronology used is based on Cunliffe (2005; 2006) and Brown (2009), approximate dates being: Earliest Iron Age (800-600 BC); Early Iron Age (600-400 BC); Middle Iron Age (400-100 BC); and Late Iron Age (100 BC-AD 50).

'Hillfort' is not a word recognised by most dictionaries; it is, however, the normal spelling in reports of Iron Age research, especially by the Hillfort Study Group, whose usage for this and other words has been adopted. With respect to slinging, it is not correct to refer to 'firing' the stone, as no fire is involved, but expressions such as 'covering fire' are used in the tactics discussion, being clearer than purist alternatives. The use of the expression 'defences' herein is not an assumption of their function; it is simply more usual than the neutral term 'enclosing works' suggested by Lock and Ralston (2013).

Chapter 2: Iron Age Hillfort Defences

As background to the experimental investigation of hillfort defences in action, this chapter describes their features, their development during the Iron Age, and the functional interpretations of the features and changes. The first section defines hillfort defences and distinguishes them from other aspects of hillforts.

Distinguishing Hillforts and Hillfort Defences

The defences are the most visible features of a hillfort, so it is not surprising that to most visitors, it appears that the defences *are* the hillfort. Archaeological survey and excavation, however, show that there is much more to a hillfort than its banks and ditches. They reveal houses and other buildings, sometimes hundreds or even thousands of storage pits and post-supported structures, roadways, burials and other depositions. Outside the hillfort are the field systems, enclosures and settlements of its community. Often hundreds of years of use and development are revealed.

There is a good deal of variability in what is found. At Danebury, the excavators estimated there had been 4200 pits, 500 rectangular structures and 130 houses in the interior of the hillfort (Cunliffe 1995: 5; Poole 1995: 262); it was occupied and developed over at least 500 years with an increasingly central role in the life of a wide area. By contrast, at Uffington Castle little evidence of settlement was found but the site appeared to have seasonal visits, perhaps as a ceremonial centre associated with the nearby White Horse (Lock *et al.* 2003).

The defences, then, could be regarded as peripheral – figuratively as well as literally – to the principal functions of the hillfort. That they must nonetheless have been important to the community is demonstrated by the effort invested in their construction and maintenance (Finney 2006: 10-11; Brown 2009: 35) and by the inconvenience of the inaccessibility they caused (Ralston 2006). In this context, it is not surprising that many archaeologists who study hillforts interpret the purpose of the defences in terms of their implications for the cohesion and prestige of the community, rather than seeing them in isolation as defensive structures.

Defensive interpretations, however, are not without supporters. They start from the fact that the ramparts, ditches and entrances have characteristics that are shared with defensive structures from other periods and locations. There is also similarity in the construction of hillfort defences of a given period, at least regionally and within the scope of the available materials, and developments occurred across sites in a recognisable pattern. The implication of these similarities of design is consistency of purpose; although the functions of the hillforts varied greatly, the functions of the hillfort defences were similar across many sites. Whether the changes over time reflect changes of function or improved approaches to the same function is discussed below.

Given the variability, why are these monuments classified as a single type: hillforts? There are numerous definitions, many of which are contradictory (Lock and Ralston 2012). However, although the size, siting, interior features and use of hillforts vary significantly, all definitions include substantial enclosing works. Despite the name, they include sites that are not on hills, but which do have the defensive features: it is the nature of the enclosure that is the determinant.

One can suggest, therefore, that there is a class of structure, 'hillfort defences,' that is not the same as 'hillforts.' It includes the banks, ditches, and entrances (and associated works such as gates and *chevaux-de-frise*). It occurs at sites whose other functions vary widely (occupation, ritual, meeting-place, crop storage, and so on). If it is defensive, it employs similar approaches to defence irrespective of what is being protected. (Or alternatively, there is similarity across sites in the ways that boundaries are marked, symbols of prestige are displayed, or social benefits from construction are achieved.) This is not meant to suggest that hillfort defences are *separate* from hillforts; they are parts of hillforts, but they are not synonymous with hillforts.

Hillfort Investigations

Hillforts have long been a focus of study for archaeologists: Lane Fox (later Pitt Rivers) determined that they were defensive sites in his survey of the Sussex hillforts in 1867 (Lane Fox 1869; Bowden 1991). Following Pitt Rivers, in the early twentieth century Maud Cunnington, E. C. Curwen, Christopher Hawkes and Mortimer Wheeler brought the number of excavated hillforts to around 80 (Cunliffe 2006: 151).

In 1931, Christopher Hawkes published a 'Retrospect' including 69 hillforts, describing their development and regional variations (Hawkes 1931). He considered their defences to be fortifications, albeit rarely-used in the early period and declining in the later Iron Age due to Belgic and Roman invasions.

In the second half of the twentieth century, the focus shifted toward the interiors of hillforts. Larger-scale excavations included Croft Ambrey (Stanford and Greig 1974), South Cadbury (Alcock 1972), Maiden Castle (Sharples 1991b) and Danebury (Cunliffe 1984a; 1995). These excavations gave much greater insight into the functions of hillforts, discussed below, especially as supplemented by broader studies of their environs, as at Danebury (Cunliffe 2000; Palmer 1984), Maiden Castle (Sharples 1991b) and South Cadbury (Tabor 2008; 2012).

More recently, excavation at individual sites has been coordinated into projects studying broader areas, such as the Ridgeway hillforts (Lock and Gosden 2002) and the Clwydian Range (Mrowiec and Gale 2007).

Development of Hillforts during the Iron Age

A deliberately-introduced change to the surrounding works of a hillfort may reasonably be assumed to either improve the structure's capability to provide its required function, or to reflect a change in the requirement. Study of the improved capabilities provided by changes, therefore, can give clues as to what the functions were. Major changes to hillforts that appear to have been common or systematic are summarised below.

General Pattern of Hillfort Development

The broad pattern of development described below is based on Cunliffe (2005: 378-406; 2006), Ralston (2006), Brown (2009) and Harding (2012).

The predecessors of hillforts, in the Earliest Iron Age, were large hilltop enclosures with modest defences, such as Balksbury (Wainwright and Davies 1995). They include a few roundhouses and a few four-post structures usually interpreted as granaries, but excavation has not generally found evidence of intensive occupation at these sites, which suggests sporadic or seasonal usage. In this period there were also undefended settlements and a few smaller enclosures with large or multiple earthwork defences, for example Lidbury Camp (McOmish et al. 2002).

FIGURE 2. HOARD OF 22260 SLING-STONES AT MAIDEN CASTLE (REPRODUCED BY KIND PERMISSION OF THE SOCIETY OF ANTIQUARIES OF LONDON, FROM WHEELER 1943, PLATE CIV, A; © RESERVED).

The Early Iron Age in southern Britain

featured contour hillforts with a single ditch and rampart, usually with two entrances. Excavations at Danebury, Maiden Castle, and South Cadbury revealed houses and storage pits from this period. Hornworks to the entrances and the use of hill-top sites, plus hoards of sling-stones as shown in Figure 2, suggest that defence was at least part of their function.

In the Middle Iron Age in southern Britain a number of hillforts were abandoned, while others were enhanced with significant increases to their defences and usage (see Figure 3). At Danebury, for example, one entrance was blocked and the other elaborated, the ramparts were increased in size and the ditch was cut into a deeper V-shape (Cunliffe 1995). Other sites in the area, such as Woolbury, Quarley and Bury Hill, appear to have become less active (Cunliffe 2006). South Cadbury, Blewburton, Maiden Castle and Hod Hill were enhanced in similar ways to Danebury in this period. Occupation increased at the developed sites, evidenced by houses, four-post structures and a high density of storage pits. There is also evidence of shrines or temples at Danebury, Maiden Castle and South Cadbury.

In the 1st century BC, a small number of hillforts with banks either side of a single ditch were built on new or previously-abandoned sites, in eastern Wessex. These 'late hillforts' include Bury Hill 2, Chisbury and Suddern Farm (Cunliffe 2006: 158).

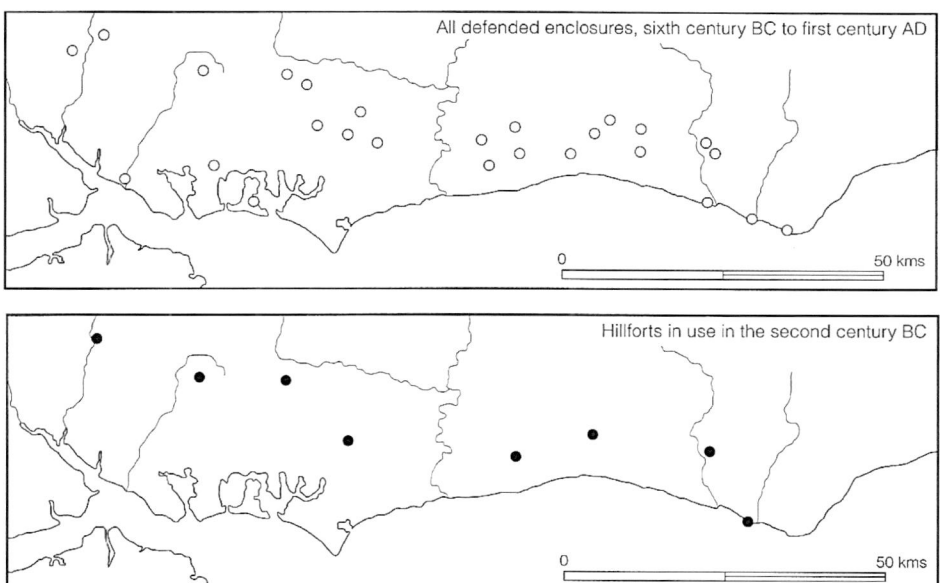

FIGURE 3. CONCENTRATION OF HILLFORT USE IN MIDDLE AND LATER IRON AGE (FROM CUNLIFFE 2005 FIGURE 15.28: 389; BY KIND PERMISSION OF BARRY CUNLIFFE).

Activities in the interiors of hillforts are mentioned only briefly here because the main topic is defences, and variations in interiors occur independently of the development of defences: *'there need be no direct correlation between the form of the fort and what went on within'* (Cunliffe 2006: 157).

Development of the Defences

Turning to the development of the hillfort defences, the following sequence is drawn from Avery (1993a), Cunliffe (2005: 348-377; 2006) and Ralston (2006).

In the hillfort-dominated zone running from Wessex up through the Welsh Marches, the general pattern starts with palisades in the 9th century BC, followed by simple box ramparts with ditches in the 7th or 6th centuries, as shown in Figure 4. Later box ramparts were supported by a sloping rampart on the inner side, and enhancements were added to the timber strengthening, such as at Moel-y-Gaer (Guilbert 1975) and at Hod Hill (Richmond 1968).

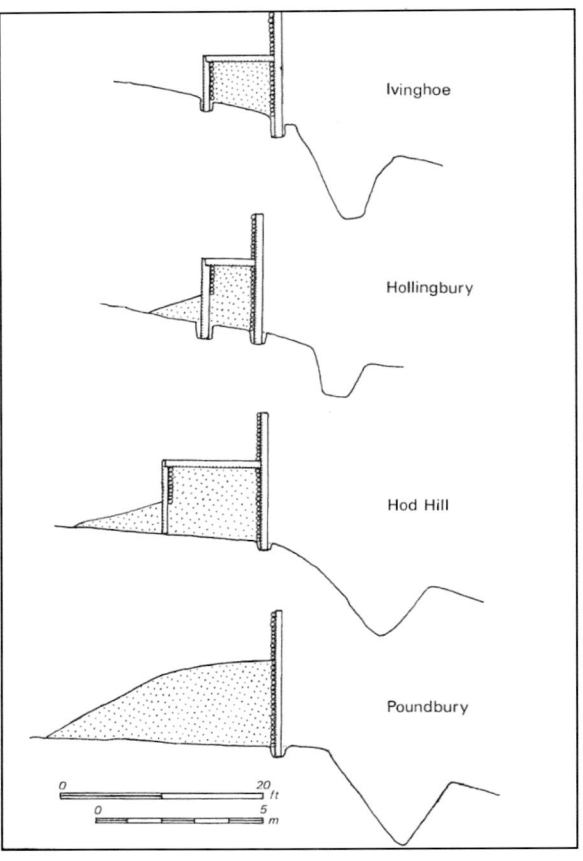

FIGURE 4. TIMBER BOX RAMPART CONSTRUCTIONS (FROM DYER 1981, FIGURE 7: 41; BY KIND PERMISSION OF ANN BODDY).

In many cases in the south these were replaced in the 5th or 4th century by glacis-style ramparts, which have continuous slopes into deeper V-shaped ditches, as shown in Figure 5, perhaps with breast works at the top; these might be further enlarged in the 3rd or 2nd century. A few sites in the 1st century BC were built as a ditch with a large bank either side. Finally, the flat-bottomed Fécamp ditch was adopted at some sites in the 1st century AD.

The above simplifies the chronology; many of the styles of rampart were in use at the same time and not all sites followed the sequence. For example, in

Chapter 2: Iron Age Hillfort Defences

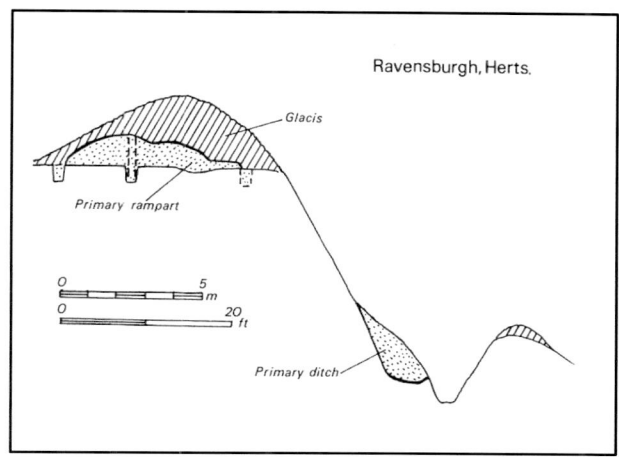

FIGURE 5. GLACIS-STYLE RAMPART
(FROM DYER 1981, FIGURE 8: 42; BY KIND PERMISSION OF ANN BODDY).

southern and eastern Britain glacis ramparts replaced box ramparts from the 4th century, but evidence of earlier glacis ramparts in the west and in Hampshire suggests that this may have been a re-introduction of an established technique (Cunliffe 2005: 357).

Multivallation appears to have arisen in different ways at different sites. At Maiden Castle, multivallation was introduced by building additional ramparts and ditches outside the existing rampart (Sharples 1994: 86). At Hod Hill, however, Richmond (1968) found that an outer ditch was added, with the spoil used to develop the existing palisaded counterscarp of the main ditch. In general, multivallation was a late development - perhaps as late as the 1st century BC at Hod Hill.

Variations

Where local materials favoured it, stone facing and stone-plus-timber structures were used or ramparts were constructed entirely in stone. Although the glacis-style rampart replaced stone faced ramparts in southern Britain, many sites remain in stone in Ireland, Scotland and Wales, such as Tre'r Ceiri, shown in Figure 6.

Where stone ramparts still stand, they commonly have a ledge on the inner side: this 'fire step' can be interpreted as a defensive feature. However, others are stepped all the way up (though always on the inside), so this could be a feature of construction; Ralston (2006: 60) shows it at Dunbeg, Co. Kerry and it can be seen at the Staigue Fort in the same area.

In Scotland, rubble-filled stone-faced ramparts with timber lacing were the most common structure, often without ditches. More than sixty Scottish sites are vitrified, where fire (usually involving the timber lacing) has fused the materials of the rampart. Opinions differ as to whether this was accidental, part of the construction, or the result of attackers using fire; post-conflict destruction appears the most likely (Harding 2004: 90-91; Ralston 2006: 143-162).

FIGURE 6. STONE DEFENCES AT TRE'R CEIRI.

Additional barriers in the form of *chevaux-de-frise* have been found at several sites, for example at Castell Henllys (Mytum 1999; Mytum 2013: 91-102). These take the form of areas of stones set upright, making approach to the hillfort more difficult; it is possible that other sites had *chevaux-de-frise* in wood (Harbison 1971). They would have hindered horses or chariots but the island position of the example at Dun Aengus, Inishmore (shown in Figure 7) implies that it was intended for men on foot, the objective being to slow down any approach.

A number of sites in the south west have widely-spaced multivallation (Figure 8), which is generally interpreted to be for the purpose of corralling cattle (Fox 1961: 46).

Entrances

The simplest type of entrance involved a passage through the rampart with a wooden gate at the inner end, hung from a vertical timber. To make the entrance practicable the ditch would be causewayed, although an oblique approach was sometimes required (Cunliffe 2005: 365). The passage was lined with wood or stone, and in many cases lengthened by an in-turn of the ramparts. In-turned entrances are often still visible, providing evidence that breaks in the defences are Iron Age features.

The fact that excavation reveals settings for vertical timbers does not prove that swinging gates were hung on them. Avery proposed an alternative 'piece gate' arrangement which involved baulks of timber being assembled to close the entrance or removed to open it (Avery 1993a: 80-81; 1993c figure 130). However, most reconstructions include leaf gates, on the basis of continental examples such as Biskupin and Altenburg bei Neidenstein (Ralston 2006: 72-73).

More complex gateways, not necessarily involving more complexity in the ramparts, include two gates, one inside the other, and dual portal entrances where the timber settings imply a two-leaf gate supported at either side. Examples include

FIGURE 7. *CHEVAUX-DE-FRISE* AT DUN AENGUS, CO. GALWAY (FROM WEIR 2013, BY KIND PERMISSION OF ANTHONY WEIR).

The Trundle and Bury Wood Camp, which are shown in Figure 9.

The development of entrances from simple gaps or in-turned ramparts involved the building of outworks that hid the gates and extended the approach to pass between ramparts, allowing defenders to be positioned above the route.

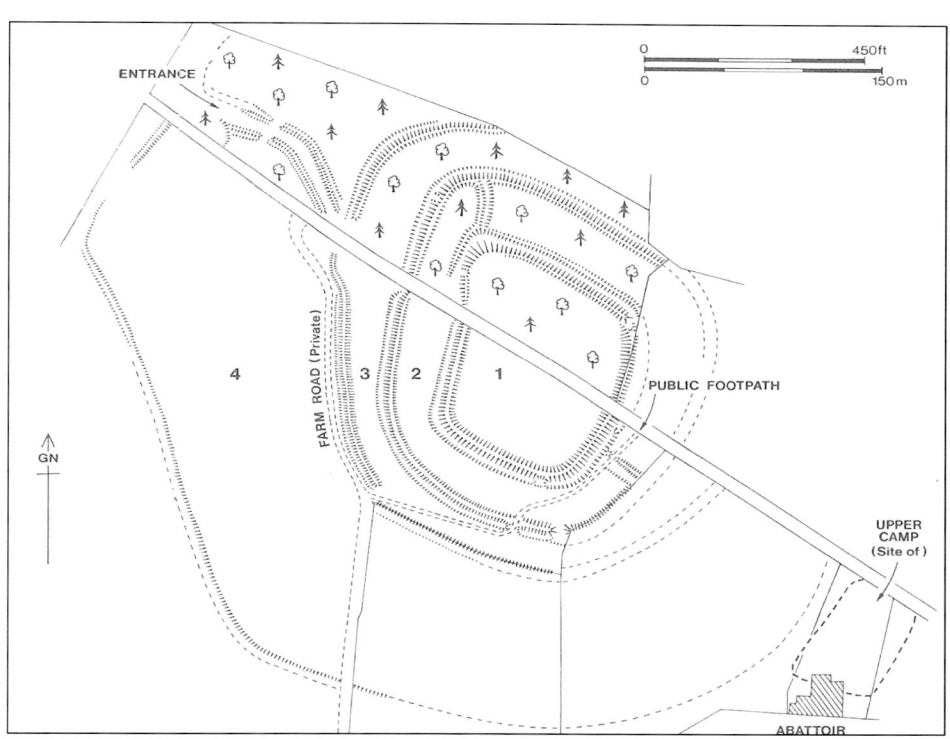

FIGURE 8. MILBER DOWN MULTIPLE ENCLOSURE HILLFORT (FROM FOX, QUINNELL AND ROUILLARD 1987: 2; COPYRIGHT DEVON ARCHAEOLOGICAL SOCIETY).

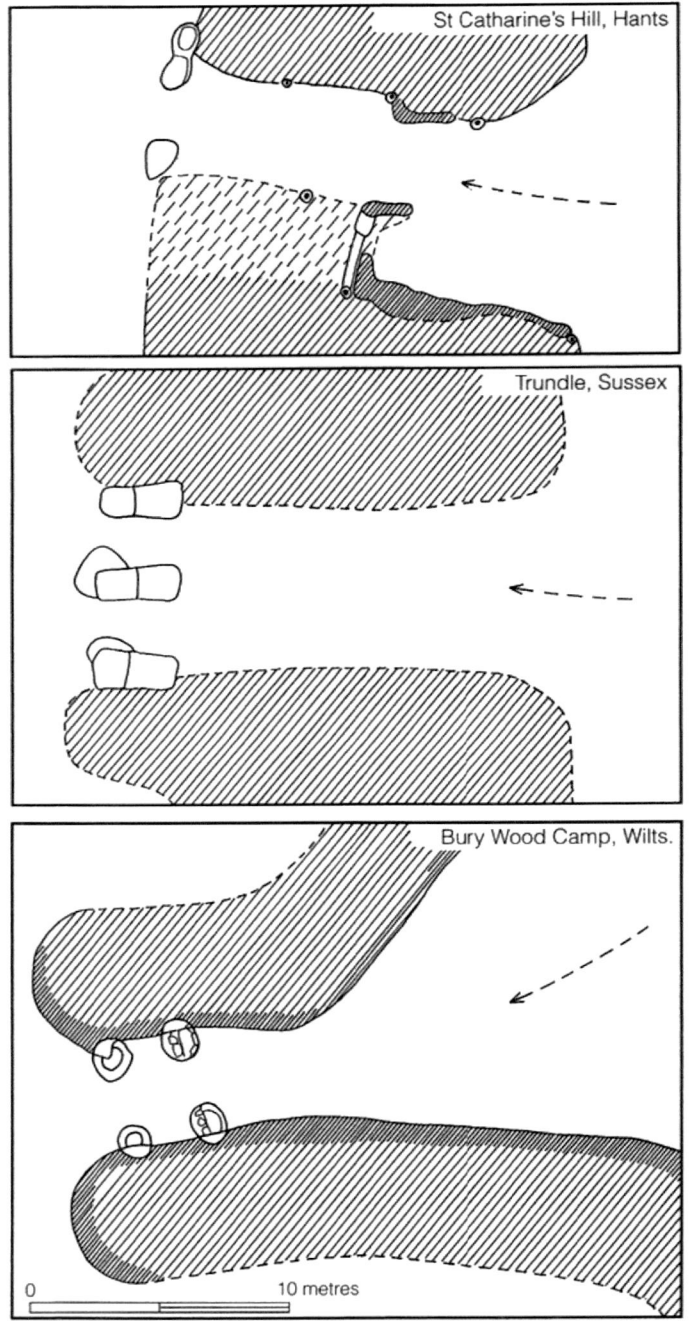

FIGURE 9. THREE IN-TURNED ENTRANCES
(FROM CUNLIFFE 2005 FIGURE 15.12: 370; BY KIND PERMISSION OF BARRY CUNLIFFE).

FIGURE 10. REMAINS OF STONE-WALL ENTRANCE PASSAGE AT MAIDEN CASTLE, SWALEDALE.

Examples of simple but large elongations of the entrance passageway occur at Torberry (Cunliffe 1976), where dry stone walls extended the passageway into the interior and at Maiden Castle, Swaledale, where a similar construction extended the passageway away from the hillfort, shown in Figure 10.

More commonly, the extension was achieved by a single earthwork that constrained the visitor to a corridor between it and the main defences. Examples include Hambledon Hill and the Steepleton Gate at Hod Hill; see Figure 11.

These designs were further elaborated at the most-developed hillforts by the addition of outer works creating longer complex routes to the entrance; Danebury and Maiden Castle (Dorset) are well-known examples. The eastern entrance to the latter is shown in Figure 11; the western entrance, shown in Figure 12, is even more complex, presenting the intruder with a maze of routes to the double entrances in the rampart. These designs also incorporated multiple gates, such as at Crickley Hill (Dixon 1994: 191).

Whereas most early hillforts had two entrances, developed hillforts tend to have had only one, the second entrance being blocked during the strengthening of ramparts, in the late 4th or early 3rd century BC (Cunliffe 2006). Corney

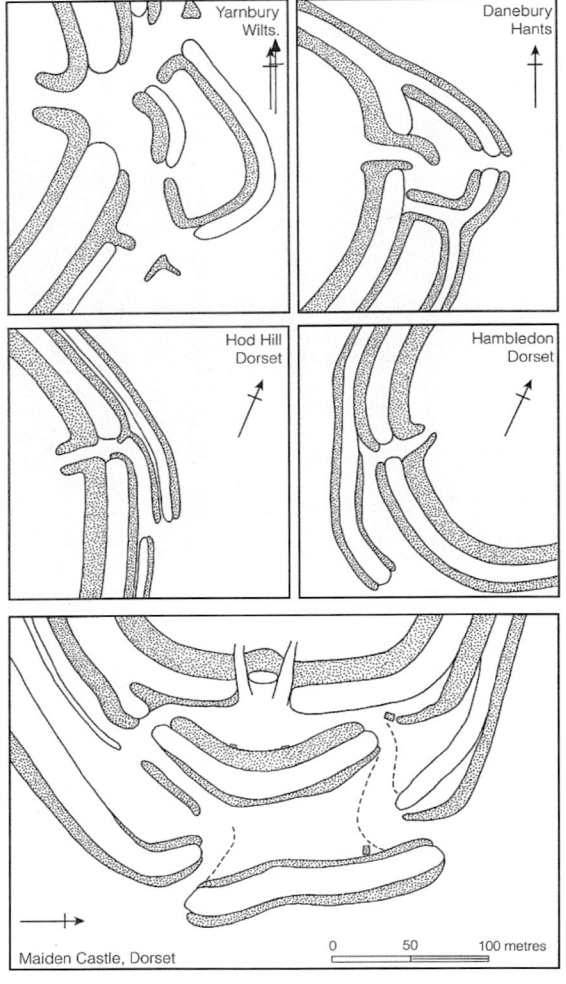

FIGURE 11. FIVE DEVELOPED ENTRANCES (FROM CUNLIFFE 2005, FIGURE 15.13, 371; BY KIND PERMISSION OF BARRY CUNLIFFE).

(2006: 138-139) discusses the evidence for fourteen such sites in Wessex and the 'kink' in defences that suggests a closed entrance can be seen at others, such as Cadbury (Devon), shown in Figure 13.

Where two entrances were present, they were typically on opposite sides of the hillfort. Single or main entrances tend to be on the eastern side (Hill 1996), the consistency of this suggesting a non-defensive purpose. However, choice of entrance position relative to the topography and directions of approach can be interpreted as defensive in a number of cases described by Ralston (2006: 40).

Variations

Guard Chambers

A number of hillforts, particularly in Wales, appear to have guard chambers built into their entrances, in the form of rooms or recesses adjacent to the passageways. It could be that more hillforts had some such arrangement but that it is more commonly preserved in the stone-built defences. That the recesses are for guards would imply security or defence as their purpose, but is by no means certain: the recesses could be for other entrance-passing functions or rites (Bowden 2006). Ralston (2006: 75) points out that access to the chambers would often be impeded by gates, when open.

FIGURE 12. MAIDEN CASTLE, DORSET, SHOWING MULTIVALLATE DEFENCES AND THE WESTERN ENTRANCE (© HISTORIC ENGLAND).

FIGURE 13. RAMPART KINK SUGGESTING BLOCKED ENTRANCE AT CADBURY, DEVON.

Bridges and Towers

Reconstructions of continental Celtic oppida often show entrance gates surmounted by bridges and towers. The evidence for towers at British hillforts, however, is thin: *'compelling evidence for such complex arrangements may need to await the recovery of a collapsed and carbonised example'* (Ralston 2006: 70). Cunliffe (2005: 373) and Brown (2009: 60) refer to evidence for bridges in the south of Britain but do not invoke towers.

Exposure of Unshielded Side

It is claimed (for example, Hill and Wileman 2002: 65; Ralston 2006: 68) that extended entrances were arranged to expose the right side of attackers to slinging, the shield being carried on the left; Karl (2008) reports that approaching left-sided was seen as threatening in Celtic societies. However, in many cases the defenders would be able to engage from either side – Figure 11 shows this, in particular with the mirror-image entrances of Hod Hill and Hambledon hillforts.

Entrances without Gates

Although gates are generally considered to have been used, conclusive evidence of leaf gates in Britain is absent. Ralston (2006: 72) interprets Caesar's comment: *'for all the entrances had been blocked by felled trees laid close together'* (*De Bello Gallico*, V, 9; Rivet 1971: 194) as an emergency measure to compensate for the lack of gates. However, Caesar does not state that there was no gate, nor that this was a response to the Roman presence; Avery interprets it as compatible with his piece-gate idea (1993a: 81), where a gate is assembled or disassembled from interlocked timbers.

Hod Hill

Hod Hill is described here to illustrate some of the points above, this being the site for the experiment reported in Chapter 5, where there are further details. The hillfort is a hill-top enclosure, roughly rectangular in shape, with defences following contours just below the summit plateau – see Figure 14. It is approximately 22ha in area. One of its special features is a Roman camp occupying the north-west corner of the Iron Age site. Figure 11 shows the main Iron Age entrance, which is also visible toward the bottom of Figure 14. Major excavations were conducted in the 1950s (Richmond 1968).

The majority of the interior is affected by ploughing, but Richmond (1968: 8) reported evidence of 240 structures, including 44 huts, palisaded enclosures and pits in an unploughed area of less than a sixth of the whole. The density of structures was confirmed by Stewart (2006; 2008): see Figure 15.

CHAPTER 2: IRON AGE HILLFORT DEFENCES   17

FIGURE 14. AERIAL PHOTOGRAPH OF HOD HILL FROM THE EAST
(© CROWN COPYRIGHT. HE).

Two of the excavated huts had sling-stone caches in their entrances, of 218 stones and 117 stones respectively. A further 887 stones were found at another hut site. Clay 'sling bolts' were also found. Earlier investigations had found *'large numbers of carefully chosen oval flint pebbles, which had been selected for slingstones (glandes)'* within a circular structure near the south east corner (Boyd Dawkins 1900: 57); these excavations found sling-stones associated with seven huts and in two other trenches. Ellis (1968: 136) suggests Chesil Beach as the source of the stones.

The construction sequence of the ramparts determined by Richmond is shown in Figure 16. In the first phase a timber-faced, chalk-filled box rampart stood above the main ditch. The ditch to rampart height of this univallate phase was about 6m. This was later converted to a glacis slope with a larger rear slope to the rampart and

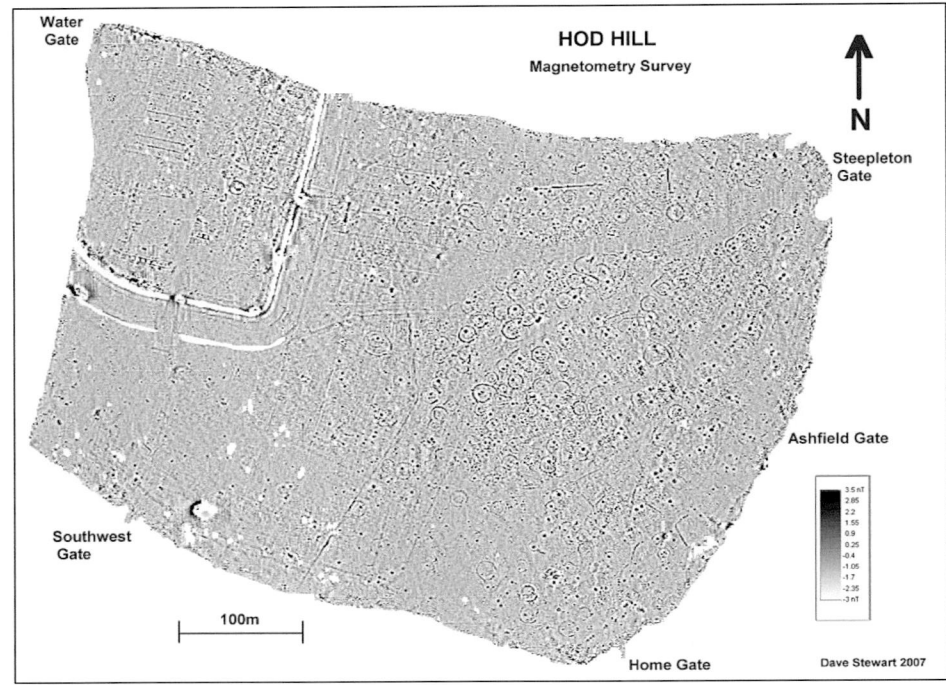

FIGURE 15. GEOPHYSICAL SURVEY OF HOD HILL INTERIOR
(COURTESY OF DAVID STEWART).

a stone breastwork, and a palisade outside the ditch. In the next phase, the main ditch was deepened, the spoil being used to create a larger counterscarp, which covered the palisade setting. Finally, the main rampart was widened and heightened and an outer ditch was dug, which Richmond believed to be unfinished.

Richmond refers to the outer bank as a counterscarp, as it was the counterscarp of the original ditch, but the three sides of the defences where this occurs are usually regarded as bivallate, with the west being univallate due to the steepness of the ground above the Stour on that side (Papworth 2011: 112). Part of Richmond's section through the northern defences is shown in Figure 17.

The Function of Hillfort Defences

Having summarised the development of hillfort enclosing works, we now turn to their function; this is the subject of some debate, the crux being whether or not they were defensive in purpose. The debate is inconclusive; it is also wide-ranging, including aspects of contemporary and Iron Age politics, psychology and metaphysics as much as it does the archaeological evidence and anthropological parallels.

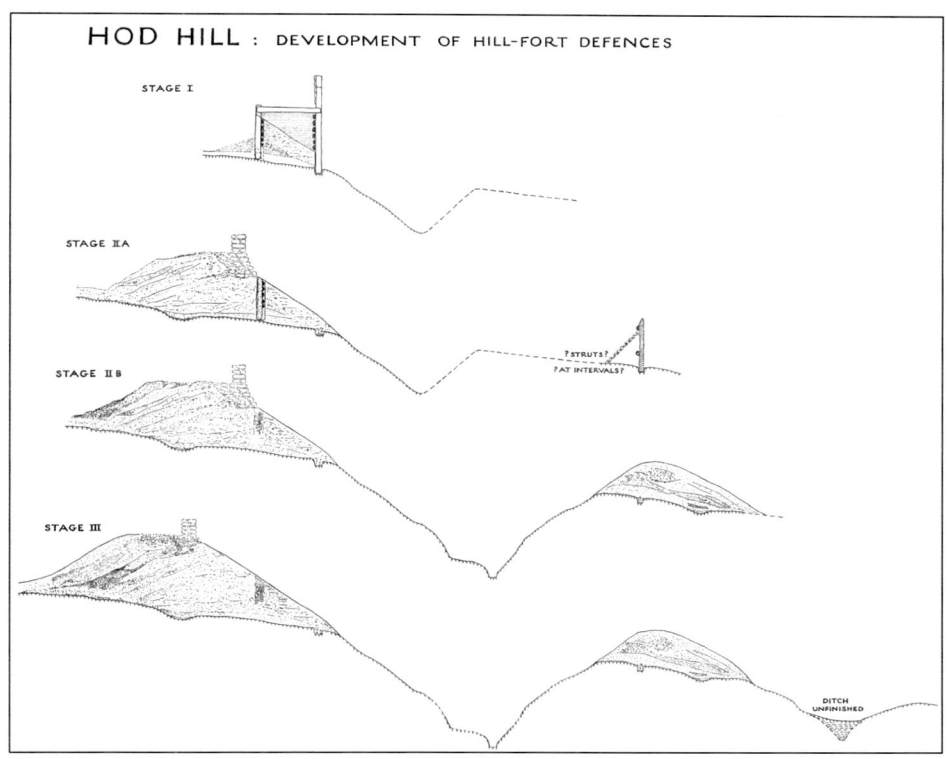

FIGURE 16. DEVELOPMENT OF HOD HILL DEFENCES
(FROM RICHMOND 1968, FIGURE 66; © THE TRUSTEES OF THE BRITISH MUSEUM).

In the early part of the twentieth century, following Pitt Rivers' lead, the function of hillforts was assumed to be defence - in the retrospect mentioned above, Christopher Hawkes' interpretation of the defences was as 'fortifications' (Hawkes 1931). This view of hillfort defences was developed at Maiden Castle by Wheeler (1943), particularly relating to sling warfare; he regarded the *breadth* of ramparts as defence against sling attacks.

John Collis related the shift to glacis construction in northern France and Britain to the rise of sling warfare (Collis 1975: 21-23), but raised doubts about endemic warfare because of sites with impressive facades but minimal rear defences, proposing that hillforts may act as symbols for the community (Collis 1996). Michael Avery (1979; 1986; 1993a) developed the idea of the relationship between hillfort defences and missile warfare, based on a tactical analysis that is described in Chapter 4 below.

Barry Cunliffe interpreted the development of particular sites and the abandonment of others (Figure 3) as indicating an increasingly centralised and hierarchical

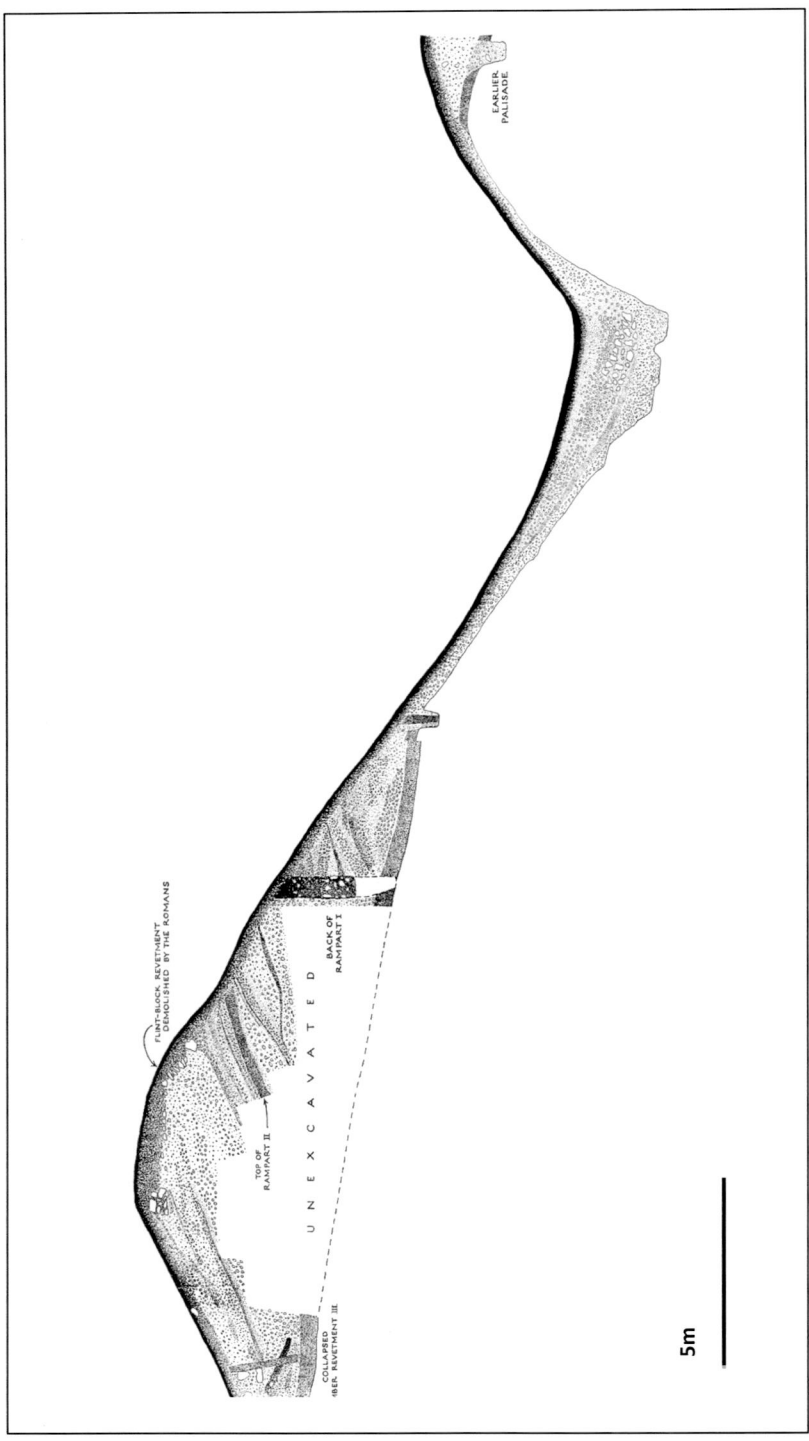

Figure 17. Section of Northern Defences of Hod Hill (adapted from Richmond 1968, figure 65; © The Trustees of the British Museum).

society, and the effort invested in hillforts as demonstrating the warlike nature of the society: *'It would be fair to say that in much of the Celtic world warfare was endemic. In central southern Britain the evidence suggests that warfare intensified as the 1st millennium progressed'* (Cunliffe 1984b: 562). Referring to defensive structures and to sling-stones found at Danebury, Timothy Darvill (1987) endorsed this. Evidence from Crickley Hill and elsewhere led him to conclude that *'the early hillforts certainly saw action'* and that *'aggression and warfare continued to be central to social relations in the later first millennium'* (Darvill 1987: 133).

Contrary interpretations that arose in the 1980s had been pre-empted by Gerhard Bersu: *'the striking fortifications of the hill-forts are only a minor element in the civilization of Iron Age A2-AB, lending it a warlike aspect which in reality it does not possess'* (Bersu 1940: 107). That not all hillfort sites were best-placed for defence was noted by Aileen Fox (1961).

Mark Bowden and Dave McOmish, in a much-cited paper, suggested that the multivallate earthworks at Maiden Castle were not practical defences, because of dead ground in the ditches and because the ditches isolated defenders of the outer ramparts; their suggested function was barriers creating social isolation and prestige (Bowden and McOmish 1987). In a later paper, they questioned the military suitability of Scratchbury and other overlooked and hill-slope sites (Bowden and McOmish 1989). These hillforts had the disadvantage that enemies could see the dispositions of defenders in the interior, which suggests that their sites were not chosen on military grounds. The same can be said of cases such as Hambledon Hill (Figure 18) where an enclosed hilltop rises above the ramparts, and where additionally a defending commander would be blind to some sides of the defences. Whether this reflects Iron Age thinking is a moot point - Finney dismissed these views as being based on modern tactics and equipment (Finney 2006: 84). To Bowden and McOmish these points supported a case for the importance of boundaries, independent of utilitarian function (Mark Bowden, personal communication).

FIGURE 18. ENCLOSED HILLTOP ABOVE RAMPARTS AT HAMBLEDON HILL.

Niall Sharples, however, suggested that warfare '*was a constant feature of the prehistoric societies of the British Isles*' (Sharples 1991a: 80) and that Bowden and McOmish's non-defensive view of hillforts was 'particularly unconvincing' (Sharples 1991b: 259); his explanation of the rise of hillforts was as protection for communities in conflicts over the control of agricultural land.

The case for non-defensive functions includes challenges to the significance of warfare in Iron Age society. Some of these stem from critiques of Cunliffe's model of increasing centralisation, hierarchy and warfare, mentioned above. JD Hill (1993; 1996) pointed out the paradox that contemporaneous undefended sites pose if hillforts had military functions; he also argued that the material culture associated with hillforts shows that their inhabitants were not elites (Hill 1995), rejecting Cunliffe's model. He suggested a society of 'dull agrarian communities' (Hill 1989: 21) of households in an 'egalitarian and boundary-obsessed' Wessex where hillforts provided special places for ritual and social functions (Hill 1996: 104-109). Similar points were made by Fitzpatrick and Morris (1994). Considering the defences as symbols, John Collis's preferred explanation was that the status being symbolised was that of the whole community, rather than of hillfort inhabitants or of 'kings' (Collis 1996: 91). The consensus appears to support the model of increasing centralisation into larger hillforts while recognising that the material evidence does not demonstrate an hierarchical society (Haselgrove 2009).

Hill (1996) also pointed out that the tendency for hillfort entrances to be to the east or the west (see Figure 19) suggests a non-functional purpose; the best defensive orientation would be different at every site.

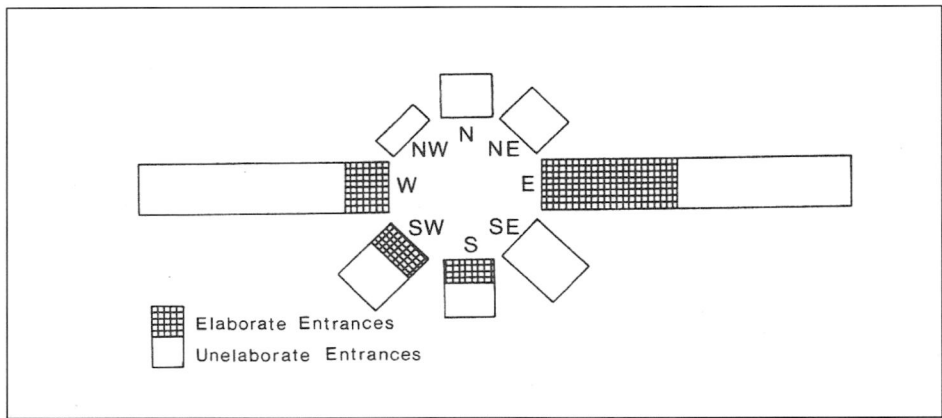

FIGURE 19. THE ORIENTATION OF 75 HILLFORT ENTRANCES IN SOUTHERN ENGLAND (FROM HILL 1996 FIGURE 8.10: 110; BY KIND PERMISSION OF JD HILL).

Although his hierarchical interpretation was weakened by the above analyses, Cunliffe's position on warfare did not change significantly over twenty years: *'while the inhabitants of Britain were in a perpetual state of endemic warfare the communities of the central southern zone probably enjoyed it to an aggravated degree'* (Cunliffe 2005: 542).

Ian Ralston (2006: 107-124) explicitly stated that the evidence for warfare is equivocal, but nonetheless Gary Lock (2007) argued that Ralston's treatment of hillforts as *fortifications* is biased by few hillfort interiors having been excavated. Accepting that hillforts were not elite residences, Lock suggested that providing boundaries was the most significant function of their defences. Lock and co-authors proposed that the main function of hillforts was to bring the community together during construction (Lock *et al.* 2005), and that *'the acts of creating and recreating such features were more important than their finished form at any point in time'* (Gosden and Lock 2007). Niall Sharples (2010: 120-124) expanded on this, proposing that mobilising resources for boundary construction was the principal medium for elite competition, the consumption of the labour being 'largely symbolic,' with emphasis on the practical and symbolic importance of the food supplies necessary to sustain construction events.

Simon James considered that the dismissal of conflict in the (Earlier) Iron Age is due to wishful thinking (James 2007), echoing Keeley's suggestion that 'pacification of the past' was due to the social context of post-war anthropologists (Keeley 1996: 174). James' examples included the near-omission of defence by Hamilton and Manley (2001) and by Haselgrove *et al.* (2001). Niall Sharples (1991a) made a similar point based on the indices of Shanks and Tilley (1987) and of Hodder (1986) - but in his own later book the main treatment of warfare is in a footnote (Sharples 2010: 265-266). James concluded that violence and insecurity were inevitably present in the Earlier Iron Age, although in his review the evidence of pathology, weapons and hillforts is ambiguous. He suggested that hillforts had a military deterrent purpose.

Ian Armit also raised objections to the 'pacification of hillforts' (Armit 2007), and criticised Lock *et al.* (2003) for ignoring the defensive character of Uffington Castle. Using Maori *pā* as a comparison, he suggested that warfare is not unusual or necessarily dysfunctional. He found the sling defence argument compelling:

> *The juxtaposition of large caches of sling-stones with defences seemingly ideal for their use . . . seems unlikely to have arisen by pure coincidence.* (Armit 2007: 33).

Gary Lock responded to Armit's paper with a critique of the claims for warfare in the Early and Middle Iron Age, suggesting that *'the communal building,* maintenance, and use of hillforts can act to structure the sociality of people whose interests are in creating a harmonious existence' (Lock 2011: 355). In this view, hillforts represent communal social expression through architecture, the hillfort defences being mechanisms for competitive display. Stressing the importance of emotion and sociality, Lock suggested that community-building explains the role of hillforts more convincingly than the 'vague' symbolic interpretation.

Most writers on both sides of this debate accept that simple single explanations are insufficient to describe all functions and implications of hillforts – they could have both defensive and symbolic effects:

> . . *deriving their form and meaning ultimately from a military exigency, but comprising a far greater range of social and cultural meaning.* (Hill and Wileman 2002: 52).

> *The hillforts do seem to be in a different category: choice of position, massiveness of defences and the sheer defensive ingenuity lavished on their entrances is sufficient to suggest that their enclosure works were designed to proclaim the strength of the occupants and to withstand attack.* (Cunliffe 2005: 364).

Warfare at Hillforts

As seen above, views on the function of hillforts provide a major part of the discussion of Iron Age warfare, and vice versa. There is evidence of burning at hillforts, described on page 35; if warfare were frequent at hillforts in the Middle and Late Iron Age, other evidence for it should be available. From Caesar we know that the Britons were capable of warfare on a considerable scale, including using hillforts (*de Bello Gallico*, IV and V.) This was centuries later, however, than the period when the majority of hillforts were being built or developed.

The use of the bow appears to be almost absent from the Middle Iron Age; no evidence for it appears in summaries of weapon finds by Avery (1993a), Finney (2006), or Cunliffe (2005) although one arrowhead was found at Danebury and another at Maiden Castle (Selwood 1984); those mentioned by Brown (2009: 105-106) are later or undated (Stanford 1984). This absence could be due to a preference for slings – Korfmann (1973) reports a polarity of choice between sling and bow in ancient times – and particularly their cost-effectiveness, especially for barrage tactics: replacing an arrow takes orders of magnitude more labour than replacing a stone.

Sling-stones apart, weapons are rare in direct association with hillforts (Avery 1993a; Sharples 1991a: 82; Finney 2006: 6) although daggers, swords, spears and javelins are known, especially from the Late Iron Age (Cunliffe 2005: 533-

534). The relatively low incidence of these weapons in the Middle Iron Age could simply be part of the low occurrence of metalwork generally (James 2007; Harding 2012), although Sharples (1991a; 2010) suggested a more complex pattern where weapons declined with the rise of hillforts.

Shields would also imply warfare, including sling warfare. The best-known Iron Age shields appear to be ceremonial or votive offerings, but may give clues to the design of common shields. Based on finds at Moel Hirradug (Brown 2009: 113) and South Cadbury (O'Connor *et al.* 2000), practical shields would be wood and leather with copper-alloy bindings and boss mounts. They could be oval in shape, but 'hide-shaped' bindings have been found at 13 sites including 5 hillforts (Stead 1991), so this may have been more common – the miniature shields from the Salisbury Hoard included both (Stead 1998).

Evidence for Iron Age warfare from trauma on human remains at hillforts is also limited. Burials with evidence of group violence have been found at Bredon Hill (Hencken 1938), Maiden Castle (Wheeler 1943), Battlesbury (Ellis and Powell 2008: 11) and South Cadbury (Woodward and Hill 2000), although Sharples' (1991a; 1991b: 100) interpretation of the Maiden Castle case is less dramatic than Wheeler's. A study of remains from Danebury concluded that there is '*ample evidence for mass-killing and mass burial*' (Craig *et al.* 2005: 176), and Bishop and Knüsel (2005) suggested that Cadbury Castle, Maiden Castle and Danebury were sites of attacks on settlements, based on analysis of juvenile/adult and male/female ratios of the human remains.

Sharples (2010: 265) disputes that this is convincing evidence for endemic warfare, but in any case most of these examples relate to Roman-period conflict (Bowden and McOmish 1987; Brown 2009: 103; Harding 2012: 182-184), an exception being that at Fin Cop (Waddington 2011a; 2011b). The pathological evidence from other burials is likewise mixed and open to widely-differing interpretations of its significance (Sharples 1991a; Craig *et al.* 2005; Armit 2007; James 2007; Redfern 2009).

The evidence from weapons and pathology, then, is too equivocal to make a strong case for frequent warfare in the Iron Age independently from the implications of hillfort architecture, especially bearing in mind the difficulty of forming judgements about prehistoric warfare (Thorpe 2005). This perhaps suggests endemic insecurity and a requirement for protection against raids, rather than full-scale war (Cunliffe 2005: 541).

Chapter 3: The Sling and Sling Warfare

This chapter describes slings and the evidence for their use as weapons during the Iron Age. It concentrates on aspects relevant to the defence of Iron Age hillforts – full descriptions of the construction and methods of using slings can be found at www.slinging.org.

Construction and Operation of Slings

The sling comprises a retention cord, a release cord and a pouch. The shot is placed in the pouch and whirled round, flying off when one cord is released, the retention cord being held in place by a finger loop. There are numerous styles of casting, such as underarm, overhead or figure-eight, which relate to the path through which the stone is given speed and brought to the point of release.

The cords in antiquity were braided from wool or plant fibres or plaited from leather strips. The pouch may be of leather, roughly lozenge-shaped, sometimes with slits to enable it to curve around the shot, as shown in Figure 38. Alternatively, it may be woven or braided from the material of the cords, as in Figures 20 and 37.

The size of the pouch and lengths of the cords vary to suit different shot or different ranges of operation. A pouch is around 15cm by 7cm (less if braided) and the length of the cords typically between 60cm and 80cm, but this may be varied according to the stature of the slinger, slinging style or required range.

Shot

Shot can be any small hard object; those used in the Iron Age were selected stones – usually river or beach pebbles – or were made from baked clay or carved chalk; cast lead was used by the Romans (Greep 1987). Manufactured

FIGURE 20. REPRODUCTION PLAITED SLING
(FROM HARRISON 2011; BY KIND PERMISSION OF ALEX JOHNSON).

shot are often biconical, as shown in Figure 21, giving consistent trajectories due to the symmetry and to the shot spinning upon leaving the pouch.

Archaeological Evidence

Sling-stones

The principal archaeological evidence for sling warfare in Iron Age Britain is the caches of sling-stones found at hillforts. Although individual stones and small groups are found, it is the large assemblages that enable them to be identified as shot. Rounded smooth pebbles in the range 19g to 172g have been found in at least 56 sites (Finney 2006).

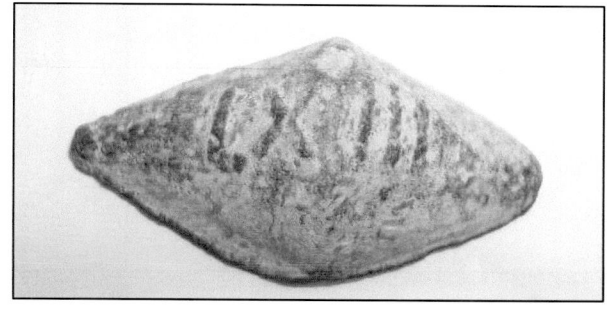

FIGURE 21. ROMAN BICONICAL SHOT
(COURTESY OF SAMI TAHA, BIBLICAL ARTIFACTS, JERUSALEM).

FIGURE 22. HOARD OF SLING-STONES NEAR EASTERN ENTRANCE OF MAIDEN CASTLE
(REPRODUCED BY KIND PERMISSION OF THE SOCIETY OF ANTIQUARIES OF LONDON, FROM WHEELER 1943, PLATE CIV, B; © RESERVED).

The largest hoards were at Maiden Castle (Figures 2 and 22), where one group of 22260 stones was found near the eastern entrance, and additionally at least 30000 others (Wheeler 1943: 49; Laws 1991: 232) and at Danebury, where one pit contained approximately 11000 and there were several thousand elsewhere on the site, including in pits close to the entrance, on the entrance works and in burials (Cunliffe 1984b: 425-6, 562; 1995: 94; Poole 1995). Over a thousand were found at Hod Hill, mainly associated with houses (Richmond 1968: 9).

At Blackbury Camp, 1271 sling-stones weighing from 57g to 78g were recovered; the greater number at the entrance (Young and Richardson 1954-5). At Moel y Gaer, Rhosesmor, '*large numbers of egg-sized water-worn pebbles*'

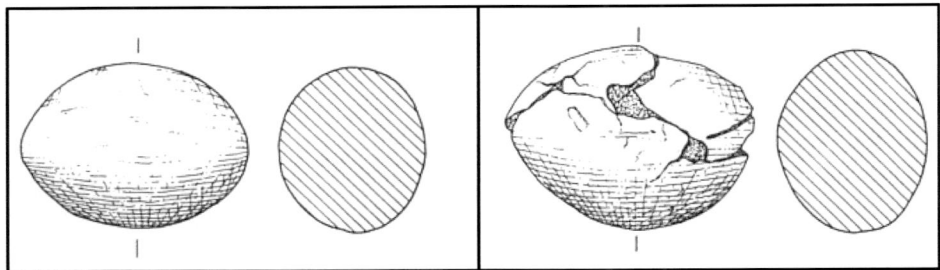

FIGURE 23. CLAY SHOT FROM DANEBURY
(FROM POOLE 1984, FIGURE 7.44, 399; BY KIND PERMISSION OF CYNTHIA POOLE AND BARRY CUNLIFFE).

were found in the rear of the ramparts and in two roundhouses (Guilbert 1975: 113). One pit near a roundhouse at Segsbury yielded 544 sling-stones (Roe 2005). At Ham Hill the 2011 and 2012 excavations, respectively, found 15.6kg and 8.7kg of sling-stones, each weighing 20-50g, including a cache associated with a roundhouse (Timberlake 2013).

Although there is a good deal of variability in the size of the stones, there appears to be a difference between sites. Typical stone sizes, interpreted from Finney (2006), were approximately: Cadbury 40g, Maiden Castle 50g, Uffington 63g and Danebury 70g.

Carved chalk and baked clay shot are found in smaller numbers; Figure 23 shows one from Danebury. They are also smaller in size: at Danebury 14 weighed from 30g to 50g (Poole 1984), while at Cadbury 113 shot averaged 18g (Poole 2000), which may indicate specialist uses, perhaps in herding or hunting (Poole 1984; 1991). Some clay shot appear to be sun-baked rather than fired; this would tend to give a heavier result (Korfmann 1973: 39; Poole 1984: 398). Modern slingers speculate that clay shot could be soaked before use, making them light to carry but heavy on impact (David Colter, personal communication).

The made shot are similar in shape to glandes known to have been made for slinging, but no author appears to have challenged the interpretation of the natural pebbles as sling ammunition, although Hamilton and Manley (2001: 26) questioned whether the stones had actually been used.

Not every hillfort excavation produces sling-stones: the excavators were 'certain' they were not used at Croft Ambrey (Stanford and Greig 1974: 44), based on absent evidence.

Slings

The organic materials of slings would not normally survive from the Iron Age. Skov (2013: 12) reports slings from North American sites contemporary with the British Iron Age, based on information from Heizer and Johnson (1952) and from York and York (2011), and some enthusiasts claim that preserved leather slings have been misidentified as parts of shoes (Alex Johnson, personal communication). Finds from later periods illustrate that this is conceivable – Figure 24 shows finds from Medieval York, which were not identified as sling pouches (Mould *et al.* 2003). Given the large numbers of stones but absence of slings from the Iron Age, further investigation of this could be worthwhile.

Skeletal Trauma

Some sling shot wounds would leave traces on the skeletons of their victims. Small depressed fractures of the skull have been tentatively identified as sling-stone wounds in a number of studies; for examples, see Andrushko and Torres 2011 or Glencross and Boz 2014. Depressed cranial fractures have been identified at a number of British Iron Age sites (Redfern 2009).[1]

Uses of Slings

The sling is not only a combat weapon; Skov (2013) gives evidence of Native American use for nine purposes, including games, rituals, herding, crop protection and various forms of hunting.

FIGURE 24. LEATHER PANELS FROM MEDIEVAL YORK
(FROM MOULD *ET AL.* 2003, FIGURE 1729: 3408;. © YORK ARCHAEOLOGICAL TRUST).

---

[1] A skull from Danebury, exhibited at the Museum of the Iron Age, has a visible wound similar to the examples in these references.

Slings are still used today to keep birds and animals from crops and for herding (Brown Vega and Craig 2009; Skov 2013). Apart from protecting flocks from predators, a stone to the flank or back of an animal will encourage it along, and a stone sent to front or side will cause a sheep to shy away and change direction.

Iron Age Britons, therefore, irrespective of warrior status, could have been familiar or even expert with the use of slings due to experience of using them for other purposes; skills that could be called into use quickly when circumstances required them.

Range of Slings

Most experimental studies of slings have concentrated on range. Finney (2006: 73), Brown Vega and Craig (2009: 1265), Harrison (2011) and Skov (2013: 46) include tables of reported ranges, from the 'world record' of 505m to modest values of less than 30m. Most commentators agree that reliable measurements, repeated over multiple trials and excluding bounces, tend to be in the 50-100m range.

Jon Finney's experiment, from which Figure 25 is taken, measured an average of 56.5m from 90 casts and had he achieved the optimum angle of release each time this would have been over 65m (Finney 2006: 112). These results, however, are from

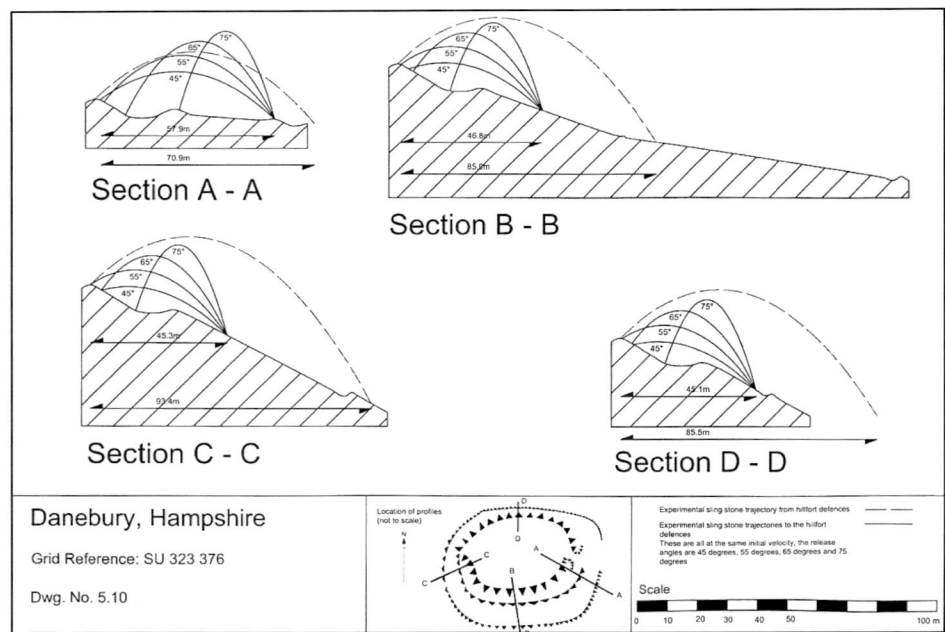

FIGURE 25. SLING-STONE TRAJECTORIES PLOTTED AGAINST HILLFORT PROFILES (COURTESY OF JON FINNEY).

a relative novice: Brown Vega and Craig (2009), prompted by Finney's work, measured the range achieved by 16 Peruvian herders of both genders who were experienced slingers; see Figure 26. Their overall average was 66m, with males averaging 78m; the modal range category for both males and females was 70-80m.

Richardson (1998) measured the range of his own casts and also estimated range from measured release velocities for various types of shot. His average for 45-75g stones was 90m.

FIGURE 26. PERUVIAN SLINGER IN TRIALS REPORTED BY BROWN VEGA AND CRAIG (2009) (COURTESY OF MARGARET BROWN VEGA).

In a recent study that builds on those predecessors, Eric Skov (2013) also measured velocity in order to compute range, for four styles and 132 casts, plus seven thrown by hand. His statistical analysis shows 'technique' (slinging style) to be a significant influence on range, although his own skill-level at the various styles will have influenced this. Unlike Finney and Richardson, Skov's calculations of range included the effect of drag, but for the highest velocity technique, 'overhand,' his computed ranges are greater, up to 170m for various projectiles – 105m for clay spheres being the most relevant to the present study.

Effect of Sling Hits

The sling was regarded in ancient times as a serious weapon (Hawkins 1847). Among the authors attesting to its effectiveness is Diodorus Siculus:

> in their assaults upon walled cities, they strike the defenders on the battlements and disable them, and in pitched battles they crush both shields and helmets and every kind of protective armour (*Library of History*, Book 5).

Livy mentions Paulus being seriously wounded by a sling bullet while fighting Hannibal (*The History of Rome*, Book 22, Chapter 49) and also describes Achaean slingers:

They used to send their stones through rings at a great distance, as targets, and were thus able to hit not only the head but whatever part of the face they aimed at. These slings kept the Samaeans from making such frequent or such daring sorties; so much so in fact that they called to the Achaeans from their walls and begged them to retire for a time and remain quiet spectators while they fought with the Roman outposts. (*The History of Rome*, Book 38, Chapter 29).

FIGURE 27. ROMAN AUXILIARY SLINGER ON TRAJAN'S COLUMN (FROM CICHORIUS 1896, PLATE XLVII).

The Roman army auxiliaries included slingers ('*funditores*'), as shown by a panel of Trajan's column, Figure 27.

Caesar mentions an injury due to slinging while fighting against the Eburones in 54 BC:

Lucius Cotta the legate received a sling wound in the mouth as he was encouraging the cohorts and centuries (*De Bello Gallico*, V: 35).

Writing in about AD 390, Vegetius also describes the effectiveness of slingers, including their value in defensive positions:

Soldiers, notwithstanding their defensive armour, are often more annoyed by the round stones from the sling than by all the arrows of the enemy. Stones kill without mangling the body, and the contusion is mortal without loss of blood. . . the sling cannot be reckoned any encumbrance, and often is of the greatest service, especially when they are obliged to engage in stony places, to defend a mountain or an eminence, or to repulse an enemy at the attack of a castle or city (*De Re Militari*, Book 1).

That penetration wounds from slings occurred is implied by Celsus' advice on treatment:

There is a third kind of missile which at times has to be extracted such as a lead ball, or a pebble, or such like, which has penetrated the skin and become fixed within unbroken. In all such cases the wound should be laid open freely, and the retained object pulled out by forceps the way it entered (De Medecina, Book VII: 4).

Finally, the sling appears in ancient literature, including The Iliad, where sling hits had a 67% mortality-rate (Pikoulis *et al.* 2004, reported by Manring *et al.* 2009), and in pre-Christian Irish myths:

Cúchulain armed with a sling and an iron ball spun his arm so fast the sling became a blur and the whirring could be heard all about the fort and then let the iron ball go so fast it went through Foill's skull and into his brain killing him instantly. (Seanchaidh 2012).

Dohrenwend (2002) reviews the biomechanical evidence for the effect of sling impacts, suggesting that fractures and penetration of the body are possible, depending on the size and shape of the projectile. His computed values for plunging fire (relevant to steeply-positioned hillfort defences) lead him to conclude the effect could '*far exceed the effect of modern military small arms*' (2002: 39). He reaches a similar conclusion for direct fire, based on roughly estimated velocities which are superseded by the measurements of Skov, reported below. Dohrenwend's discussion of tactics is not related to the defence of hillforts, although he remarks on the advantages of height, and credits Mahr (1964) with the idea that slingers fell into two categories: trained and expert slingers on one hand, and 'relatively untrained peasants' on the other, which mirrors the suggestion arising from Finney (2006) that the ultimate defence of a hillfort might rely on slinging by the general populace.

Eric Skov's recent dissertation includes a comprehensive review of ethnographic evidence of trauma due to slinging (Skov 2013). This plus biomechanical and medical evidence lead him to conclude that three types of injury can occur from sling-stone impacts: fractures, soft tissue blunt trauma and penetration. His technical analysis of the impact forces of shot compared to injury thresholds shows that skull fractures can be expected; for example, a 55g biconical clay projectile would cause fracture or unconsciousness, depending on where it hit. Penetration wounds are shown to be less likely, although possible for lead and biconical shot.

For soft tissue trauma, Skov's analysis shows the sling hits to be in the 'low lethality' zone of the graph for human-sized targets but with injuries such as liver fracture likely. Various methodological issues, however, preclude this evidence from being conclusive.

Accuracy

Striving for range reduces accuracy, of which the range experiments referred to above take no account. Massed barrages of stones against large groups of enemies would not require fine accuracy, but it would be important in situations such as hunting or animal-herding, or in smaller conflicts.

Like the Achaeans reported by Livy (above), the Balearics achieved accuracy through long practice:

> *And they are so accurate in their aim that in the majority of cases they never miss the target before them. The reason for this is the continual practice which they get from childhood, in that their mothers compel them, while still young boys, to use the sling continually; for there is set up before them as a target a piece of bread fastened to a stake, and the novice is not permitted to eat until he has hit the bread.* (Diodorus Siculus, *Library of History*, Book 5).

From the results of modern Balearic slinging competitions it appears that a regular slinger hits a 50cm diameter target more than half the time, at distances between 20m and 40m (Federacio Balear de Tir de Fona 2012). This suggests that the sling would be an effective weapon for individual combat at distances similar to the breadth of hillfort defences.

Tactics of Sling Warfare

Most reports of sling tactics relate to open battle or marine engagements (Dohrenwend 2002) and are of limited relevance to the defence of hillforts. Caesar, however, describes the use of stone missiles in an attack on the hillfort at Bibrax:

> *The Gauls and the Belgae use the same method of attack. They surround the whole circuit of the walls with a large number of men and shower it with stones from all sides, so that the defences are denuded of men.* (*De Bello Gallico*, II, 6).

On that occasion, there were '*such huge numbers throwing stones, no defender could keep his footing on the wall*' but overnight, Caesar sent reinforcements including Balearic slingers, whose arrival inspired the defenders to take the offensive (*De Bello Gallico*, II, 6-7). On a later occasion, the Gauls used slings and fire to attack the Roman legion under Cicero:

> *On the 7th day, in a high wind, they began throwing hot sling-bullets of softened clay and fire darts. These set fire to the thatched buildings.* (*De Bello Gallico*, V: 43).

There is good reason, therefore, to believe that slings were used in Iron Age conflicts at hillforts.

Chapter 4: Background to the Experiment

Few of the participants in the debate about the function of hillfort defences discuss tactics in any depth; the main exception to this is Michael Avery (1979; 1986; 1993a; 1993b). He proposed a rationale for the development of multivallation, dump ramparts and complex entrances based on tactics in which sling warfare figures prominently. (He also included the use of missiles thrown by hand.)

Avery's analysis is based on Caesar's description, quoted above, of barrages of stones followed by firing the gates. His explanation fits the observed development of defences during the Middle Iron Age, as summarised below based on Avery (1993a).

Wall and fill ramparts presented a steep face which gave significant advantage to defenders in hand-to-hand combat using spear and sword. However, wood-faced ramparts proved vulnerable to attack by fire, resulting in the development of 'low dump' ramparts which were without this disadvantage. To overcome these defences, assailants then developed the tactic of attacking entrances by stoning – weakening the defenders before engaging hand-to-hand. The tactical advantage of attack by stoning would apply to stone-faced ramparts in the same way as for dump ramparts. From this in turn developed the tactic of defence by stoning; in time, *'permanent, densely occupied sites in Wessex and the Welsh Marches took to defence by stoning and exploited it with the full development of height and breadth'* (Avery 1993a: 64). That is, the larger dump ramparts and multivallation of developed hillforts were specifically designed to give advantage to defenders in sling warfare.

That fire was used is suggested by many sites showing evidence of burning, even excluding the vitrified forts. Both entrances at Danebury have evidence of burning in the fourth century, the east entrance being burnt again *c.* 100 BC (Cunliffe 1984a: 43; 2005: 541). Brown (2009: 67) refers to examples of fired hillforts that are 'too numerous to mention' but does mention eight; Avery (1993a) refers to 35 cases of burning.

Avery proposes a similar rationale for the evolution of entrances from simple gateways to complex structures, suggesting that the tactics first developed at entrances:

> *Once, however, the importance of burning down the gate was appreciated, defenders lengthened their entrance passages, attackers realised that a preliminary stone barrage was essential and missile warfare was born as an attacking stratagem of 'stoning and fire'.* (Avery 1993: 91).

Slings were more useful weapons for attackers, who had more freedom of position and movement than defenders, because *'missiles are effective only where a dense barrage can be organised against a compact target which is relatively stationary'* (Avery 1993a: 143), but of course developed entrances with long passageways and surrounded forecourts countered this advantage by constraining attacking forces.

The dimensions of the defences at the sites that Avery (1993a; 1993b) reports may be condensed as follows. Upright-timbered and wall-and-fill ramparts were relatively low – fitting the requirement to provide an advantage in hand-to-hand fighting – that is, rarely more than 2m high. They would, however, be behind a ditch of at least 2m depth and be surmounted by a parapet. From the bottom of the ditch an attacker would face a slope of 4.5m to 6m to the berm below the parapet and then up to 2m to the lip of the parapet.

Low dump ramparts, likewise, were mostly in the range 1-3m in height, with ditches most commonly between 2m and 4m in depth. The 34 cases reported by Avery have much variation, but in general the dimensions are similar to the wall-and-fill cases.

For the 25 High and Extra High Dump ramparts listed by Avery, the ramparts are mostly between 2.5m and 5m in the High case and 4m to 5.5m in the Extra High; see Figure 28 for an example. The accompanying ditches were mostly in the range 2m to 5.5m deep, with three being 8.5m or 9m deep.

In close combat, Avery suggests that the smaller height differences would give a 2:1 or 3:1 advantage to defenders; at 4 or 5 metres it would grow to 5:1 or 10:1, but less if the slope were climbable in a rush – to prevent this, the slope needs to be 50 or 60 degrees. Attackers would also have problems retreating up the inner face of an outer bank, making the ditch a killing zone.

FIGURE 28. HIGH DUMP GLACIS RAMPART AT HAMBLEDON HILL.

Jon Finney (2006) also examined the tactical relationship between slinging and the design of hillfort defences, by surveying the profiles of 20 hillfort defences and plotting sling-stone trajectories against them: Figures 25 and 29 show examples. Section 'D-D' of Finney's survey at Hod Hill, Figure 29, is close to the site of the experiment reported below, and shows that a slinger on the inner rampart of Hod Hill could engage opponents at over 78m distance, but attacking slingers would be effective only within about 51m. Finney concluded that:

> *The evidence from the field survey seems strongly to suggest that the use of multivallation does have a significant effect on the ability of an assailing force to use the sling, if it is accepted that the areas between the banks and ditches were allowed to regenerate with scrub. At none of the multivallated hillforts surveyed would it have been possible, from the evidence provided by the experimental data, to have struck the innermost bank without entering a space defined by the outer works.* (Finney 2006: 80).

There are, however, some caveats to be mentioned. The first is that Finney's conclusion results from his own measurements of range, which are probably underestimates for experienced male slingers, as discussed on page 31; therefore slinging from outside the defences might have been somewhat effective. Secondly, his suggestion of ineffectiveness *within* the defences relies on the unproven presence of scrub and also assumes an underarm slinging style.

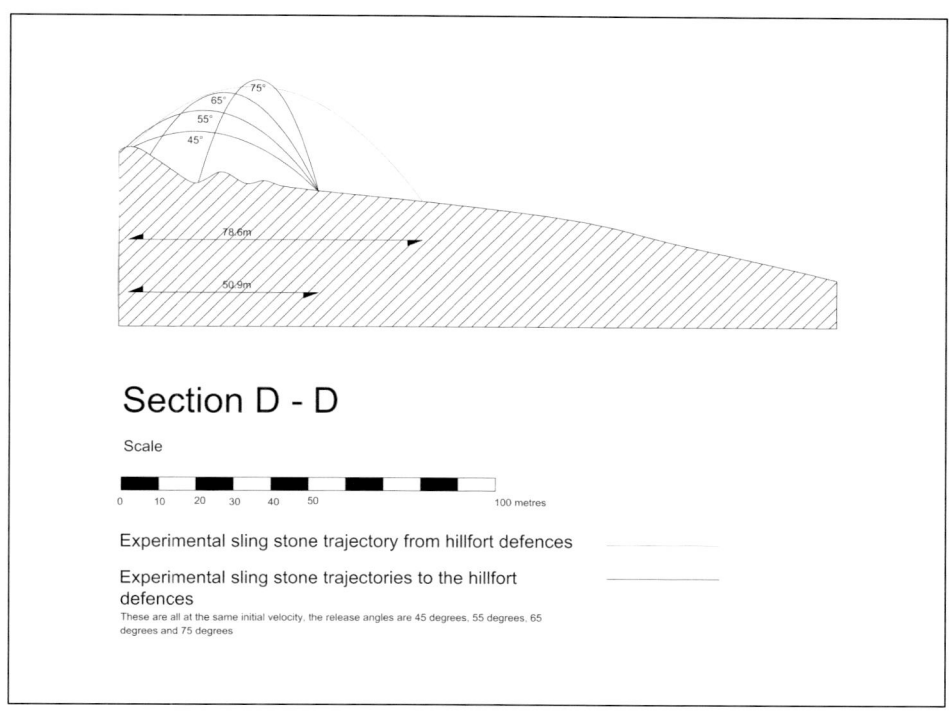

FIGURE 29. SLING-STONE TRAJECTORIES PLOTTED AGAINST THE NORTHERN DEFENCES OF HOD HILL (COURTESY OF JON FINNEY).

Finney also includes the sling in an ethnographical analysis of the social significance of Iron Age weapons, based on the myths of several cultures including pre-Christian Ireland. He shows the sling to have been a low-status tool or weapon. This conclusion is supportable from a practical perspective: slings are easily made and ammunition can be picked up from the ground. It is therefore a weapon that the common man, and woman, could use in defence of the home or settlement.

Finney proposed a model of a ritual cycle of formalised warfare (2006: 88), which is not supported by evidence such as identified battle sites. However, his observation that the sling could be used by everyone leads to the idea that the whole community would be mobilised to use slings in defence when required.

As mentioned in Chapter 3, little other information on sling performance in the context of hillforts is available, with reliable accuracy data being absent.

To sum up: there is a paucity of direct evidence relating the features of hillfort defences to their function, and little tactical analysis behind the discussion of their possible defensive function. However, the best available analysis suggests that the *changes* made to defences as hillforts developed would have improved their capabilities against attack by slings. There are no reliable measurements of the accuracy of slings in circumstances like the defence of hillforts. Addressing these gaps, therefore, provided the rationale for the experiment.

Chapter 5: The Experiment

The experiment was intended to measure the performance of slingers on bivallate dump rampart defences and on univallate defences, providing quantified results as input for tactical analysis.

Approach

The approach employed for the experiment was straightforward: a number of slingers cast stones at a target placed at selected points on the ramparts of a hillfort. The positions of the slingers and the target were arranged to represent both attack and defence of a single rampart with an outer ditch and of bivallate dump ramparts and ditches. The number of hits on the target and slinging speed were used to compare performance across slinging positions.

Practical Issues

Practical issues arising during the experiment resulted in modifications to the methodology; in some cases providing insights into the deployment of slings. The issues are reported here as explanation for the variations in method described later.

Availability and Skills of Participants

An experimental design based on eight slingers was selected, as the pilot trial showed that eight would provide enough statistical sensitivity, and more than eight practitioners had been identified. The pilot also showed that slingers could complete the trials in about 5 hours, operating singly or in pairs

In practice, only seven slingers were able to participate and four attended as a group with limited time, leading to an incomplete set of measurements being gathered. The number of measurements was made up by Participant 1 returning and completing four extra sessions, but necessarily not in a balanced order.

It was evident from the first experimental session that the participants had difficulty slinging downhill, contrary to the expectation of advantage due to height. This is apparently due to unfamiliarity – the release-point for the sling is established by training on level ground - but is unrepresentative of the Iron Age situation where the defenders could practice at the hillfort. In later trials, participants were asked to practice in both directions before slinging for score commenced.

Sling-stones

The ammunition used for the Pilot Trial and first session of the experiment was selected rounded pebbles within the size range found in hillfort excavations. These worked well in the Pilot Trial, but in the first session of the experiment the force of slinging buried several stones in the soil on the rampart. Un-retrieved stones would corrupt the archaeological record and the experiment was therefore suspended until the ammunition could be changed.

The remaining trials for Participants 1 and 2 used golf balls as ammunition. Their lower density prevented them being buried but also meant that they flew differently than stones - the slingers reported that at longer ranges the golf balls did not fly straight.

Clay ammunition was adopted for the remainder of the experiment, roughly shaped by hand and air dried. The benefit of air-dried clay is that any lost stones would dissolve away in rain. (This was informally trialled.) The slingers rated the clay shot as equal to or almost as good as stone. More details are given under 'Equipment' below.

Weather

The experiment was conducted in March 2013, which happened to be particularly cold and windy. Only one session was cancelled altogether, but slinging while wearing gloves and bulky clothing and with cold fingers must have affected the results and accelerated tiring. The wind also damaged the target, and incidentally the stopwatch while handling the target.

Phased Approach

Prior to the main experiment, earlier phases contributed information to its design and to secondary questions:

Qualitative Phase: This included review of surveys and numerous visits to hillforts, several with expert slingers. The results influenced the procedure and also fed into the tactical analysis.

Informal Trials: These were used to test the experimental procedure and provide estimates of timing and hit-rates. Alternative target arrangements, the choice of stone size and shape to be used, and the impact effects of hits were also assessed. A trial of the time to make an assault of the ramparts was run at Hod Hill, as was an informal trial of effective range.

Pilot Experiment: This confirmed and refined the procedure. The pilot also gave data on variability of results, confirming the statistical design.

Chapter 5: The Experiment

Experiment Method

Site

The main experimental conditions aimed to represent a bivallate dump rampart hillfort and a univallate hillfort with a box rampart. No faced rampart with bivallate ramparts nearby was found, so it was decided to use a bivallate hillfort with a section of outer rampart representing the univallate case. Hod Hill was chosen because of its bivallate ramparts and relative ease of access. The location of Hod Hill is shown in Figure 30,[2] and a general description of the hillfort is given above, on page 16.

Aerial views of the site are shown in Figures 14 and 31. the experiment site was at the western end of the northern defences, to the left of the path visible in Figure 31. The ramparts used for the experiment are shown in Figure 32.

One line of slinging ('bivallate') crossed both ramparts and ditches; the other ('univallate') crossed just the outer rampart and ditch, as shown in Figure 33.

The work was carried out under a formal research agreement with The National Trust, who own the site. This included conditions to ensure public safety and care of the site, which were incorporated into the experiment procedure and safety plan, described below.

Survey

The profiles of the slinging lines were surveyed using level, staff and tape, and the 'through the air' distances between the slinging and target positions were also measured by tape. The profiles are shown in Figures 34 and 35.

In the univallate case the rampart top is 4.3m above the bottom of the ditch and 3.2m above the counterscarp, and the rampart slope is approximately 29° overall. In the bivallate case, the outer rampart top is 4.6m above the bottom of the outer ditch and 3.6m above the counterscarp, with a slope of approximately 27°, and the inner rampart top is 9.0m above the bottom of the inner ditch and 4.8m above the outer rampart, with a slope of approximately 31°. The maximum horizontal range required of the slingers was approximately 20m in the univallate case and 46m in the bivallate case.

---

[2] The maps in Figures 30 and 33 were created using OS VectorMap® Local [SHAPE geospatial data], Scale 1:10000, Tiles: st80nw,st80ne,st81sw,st81se, Updated: 1 October 2015, Ordnance Survey (GB), Using: EDINA Digimap Ordnance Survey Service, <http://digimap.edina.ac.uk>, Downloaded: 2015-11-20 12:32:10.085 and OS VectorMap™ District [SHAPE geospatial data], Scale 1:25000, Tiles: st, Updated: 9 September 2015, Ordnance Survey (GB), Using: EDINA Digimap Ordnance Survey Service, <http://digimap.edina.ac.uk>, Downloaded: 2015-11-20 12:32:10.085. Reproduced under OS Open Data Licence, see http://www.nationalarchives.gov.uk/doc/open-government-licence/version/3/.

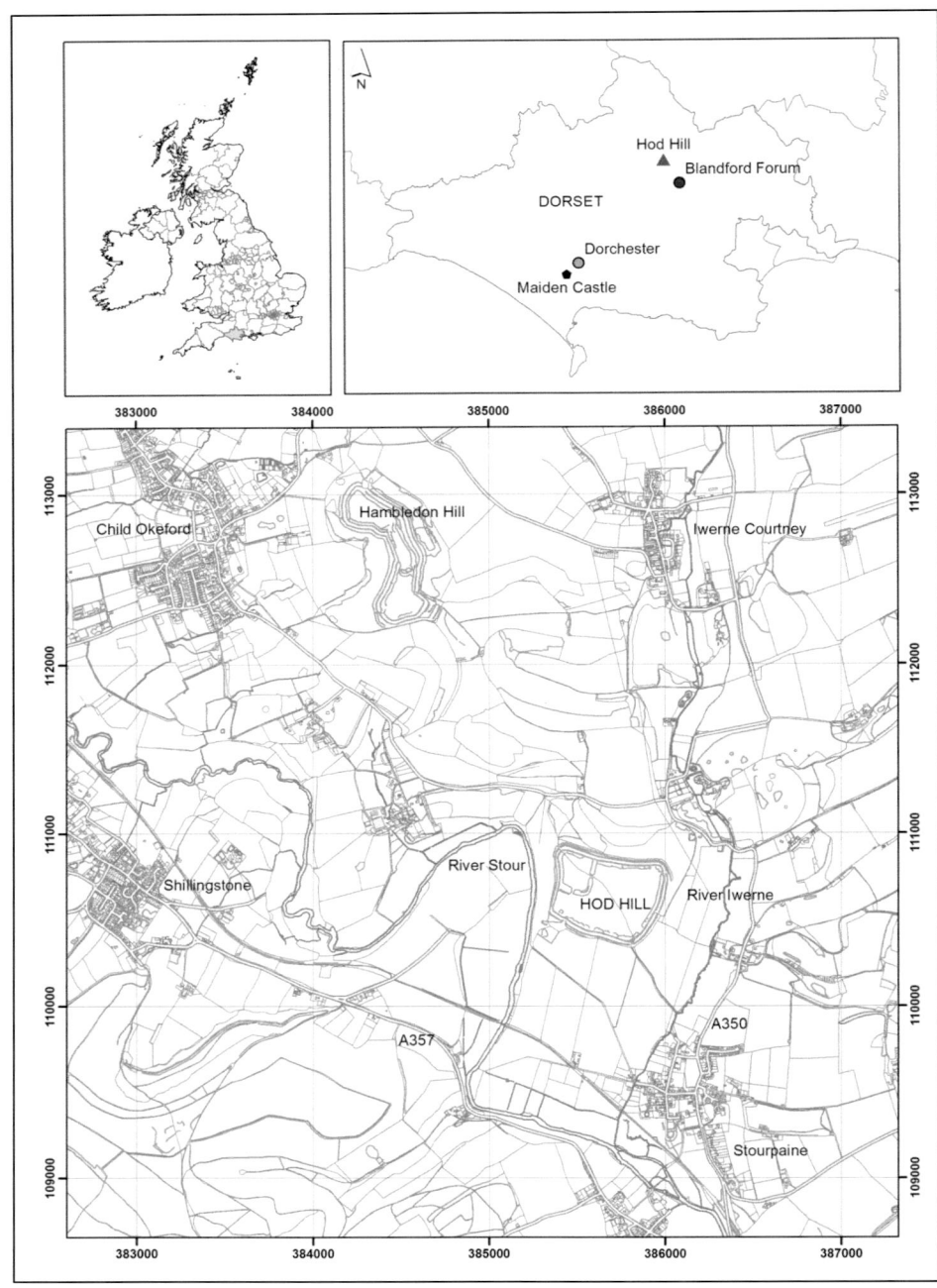

Figure 30. Location Map for Hod Hill
(map created using OS VectorMap® Local, reproduced under OS Open Data Licence).

FIGURE 31. AERIAL VIEW OF HOD HILL FROM THE WEST; EXPERIMENT SITE IS BOTTOM-LEFT
(© HISTORIC ENGLAND).

Experimental Conditions and Variables

This section summarises the experimental conditions and gives the rationale for exclusion or control of other candidate conditions and variables.

1. Single rampart versus bivallate ramparts

These main conditions were achieved by using the selected profiles of the defences. No attempt was made to separately trial rampart form and bivallation.

2. Attack versus defence

Attack and in defence were treated as main conditions.

3. Distance of attackers from rampart

FIGURE 32. INNER RAMPART AND DITCH OF HOD HILL, SEEN FROM OUTER RAMPART.

The assumed model for an assault is that the attackers move from the distance across the outer earthworks and attempt to scale the rampart. This was simulated by placing the target at key points in the approach, to examine the defenders' performance as the assault proceeded. In the case of the slinger attacking, he stood at those positions and cast at the target on the rampart. The positions were trialled from the outside working inwards in each case.

Nine 'attacking' positions were used, each representing a section of the defences. Seven apply in the bivallate case and five in the univallate case:

1. Beyond the outer earthworks
2. On the counterscarp bank
3. On the outer face of the outer ditch (univallate only)
4. In the outer ditch
5. On the outer face of the outer rampart (univallate only)
6. On the outer rampart (bivallate only)
7. On the inner face of the outer rampart (bivallate only)
8. In the inner ditch (bivallate only)
9. On the outer face of the inner rampart (bivallate only).

4. Single or grouped attackers

Slinging stones at a group of attackers gives an increased chance of a hit. This factor was incorporated by the target representing both a single opponent and a group.

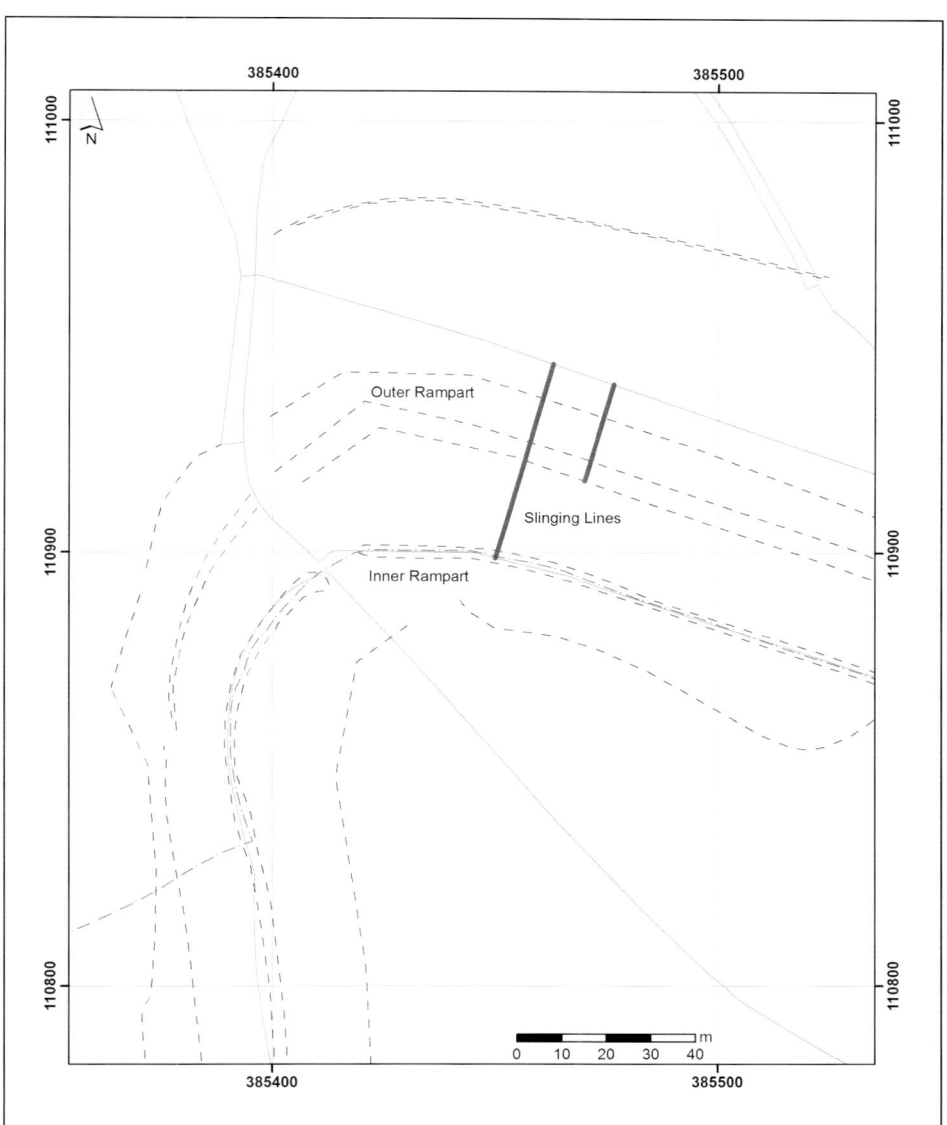

Figure 33. Plan of North-West Section of Hod Hill, Showing Slinging Lines (plan created using OS VectorMap® Local, reproduced under OS Open Data Licence).

Excluded Conditions

The following factors were excluded to keep the experiment manageable.

Slope of underlying hill: many hillforts incorporate slopes into the defences, giving defenders greater height and visibility. However, this was 'built in' to the choice of an actual hillfort site.

Sling type and slinging style: the participants used slings of their own choosing. Their slinging techniques are discussed under 'Qualitative Results.'

Sling-stones: including different sizes and materials of ammunition (stone, baked clay, or carved chalk) would be of interest, but would require more time. Although practical issues resulted in the use of three types of ammunition, this was not part of the experimental design.

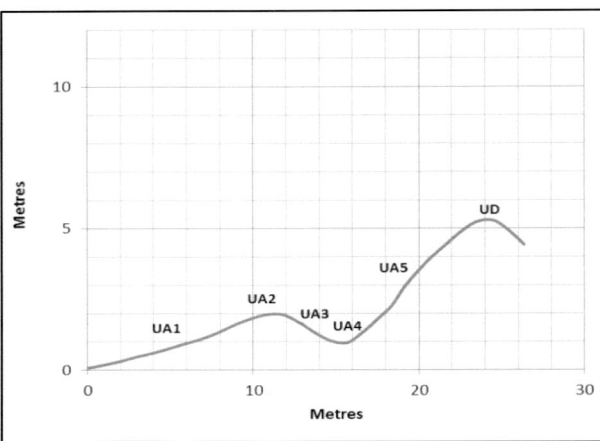

FIGURE 34. UNIVALLATE PROFILE AND SLINGING POSITIONS (VERTICAL SCALE EXAGGERATED).

Measurements

The principal measures were:

a. Accuracy, scored as hits on three parts of the target – hit pocket net ('head hits'), hit inner target ('hits'), hit outer target ('net hits') - or miss.
b. Time to complete six casts.

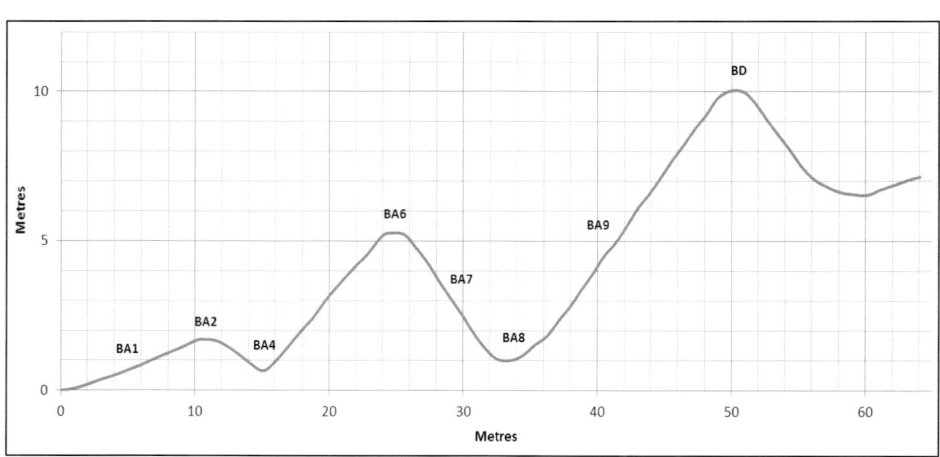

FIGURE 35. BIVALLATE PROFILE AND SLINGING POSITIONS (VERTICAL SCALE EXAGGERATED).

The experimenter also noted 'near misses' within a metre or so of the target and misses due to shot falling short. Participants' comments on the slinging positions and procedure were noted.

Repeated Measures Design

The statistical design required each participant to perform all of the experimental conditions, rather than comparing 'experimental' and 'control' groups. This has the advantage of balancing variability in the skill of the slingers across the conditions. As described above, practical issues interfered with the completion of several sessions; the details can be seen in '5.3 Results.'

The order in which participants experienced the conditions was balanced, to avoid practice or fatigue effects favouring one condition over another. The instructions encouraged accuracy throughout.

The ordering of the four main conditions was randomly assigned to participants according to the experimental design for multiples of four participants shown in Figure 36. Participants completed attack and defence of a given rampart before switching to the other, leaving only attack/defence and rampart-type to be ordered.

Participants

Seven volunteers were recruited from organisations which practice slinging for recreational or re-enactment reasons (two from *Slinging.org*, four from *Brigantia* and one from the Hillfort Study Group).

Details for each participant were recorded, including slinging experience, stature, arm and sling length, handedness and vision. These records are shown in Figure 74 in Appendix B.

Participant	Session				Order Name
	1	2	3	4	
1	Attack Outer Rampart	Defend Outer Rampart	Attack Inner Rampart	Defend Inner Rampart	UA First
2	Defend Outer Rampart	Attack Outer Rampart	Defend Inner Rampart	Attack Inner Rampart	UD First
3	Attack Inner Rampart	Defend Inner Rampart	Attack Outer Rampart	Defend Outer Rampart	BA First
4	Defend Inner Rampart	Attack Inner Rampart	Defend Outer Rampart	Attack Outer Rampart	BD First

FIGURE 36. REPEATED MEASURES EXPERIMENTAL DESIGN.

Participant 1 volunteered to return for further trials, during which he completed two complete runs, slinging double sets – twelve stones per position. These sessions were scored as if from four participants, referred to in the results as Participant 1A to 1D.

Experience of Slingers

The participants were between 24 and 50 years of age and had between 10 months and 28 years' experience with slings. Only Participants 1 and 2 could be regarded as 'regular' slingers; some had only a few previous slinging sessions. A practice session for each slinger was observed to confirm safe control of the stones.

Casting Style

The slingers were allowed to use their own judgement in choosing the casting style, allowing for different styles to suit the different conditions.

Equipment

Slings

Participants used their own slings; details are given in Appendix B. The majority were of 'traditional' design and materials, with leather pouches and cords of plaited leather thong or jute string. One was of Andean design from braided alpaca

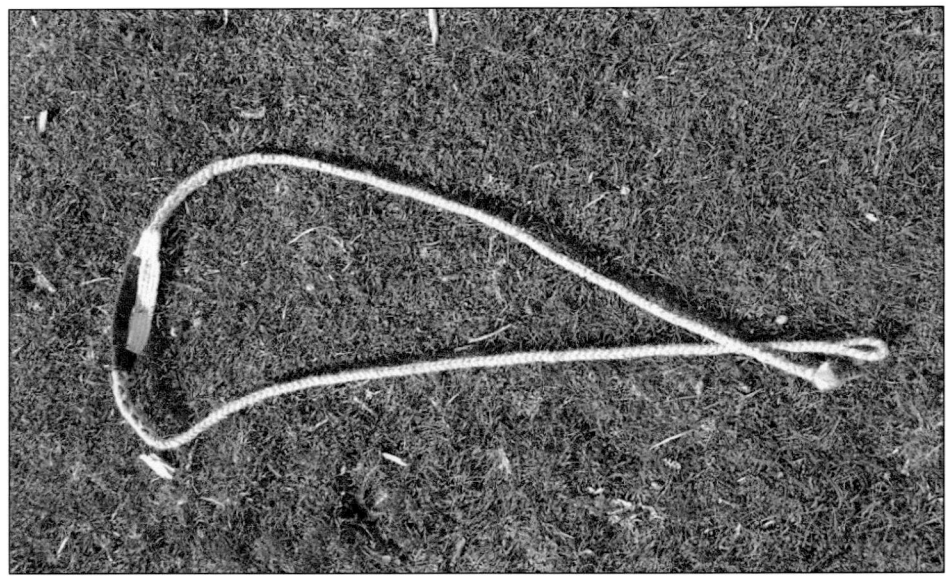

Figure 37. Andean Sling.

Chapter 5: The Experiment

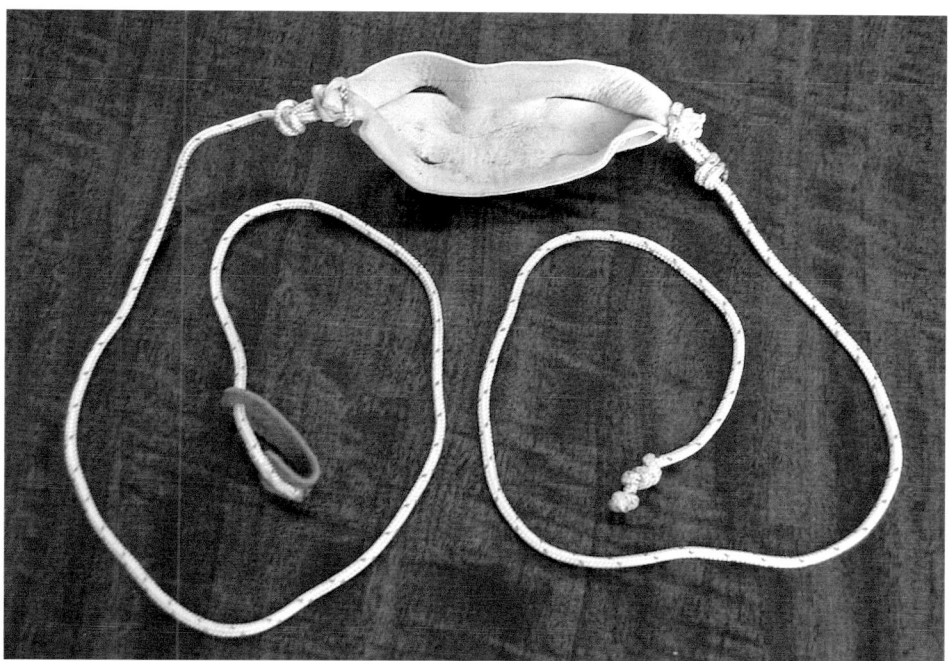

FIGURE 38. MODERN SLING SIMILAR TO ONE USED IN THE EXPERIMENT.

wool with an integral split pouch; it is shown in Figure 37. Figure 38 shows a modern example and Figure 39 shows a staff sling, approximately 1m long, which was constructed impromptu on site and used in the trial of effective range.

Sling-stones

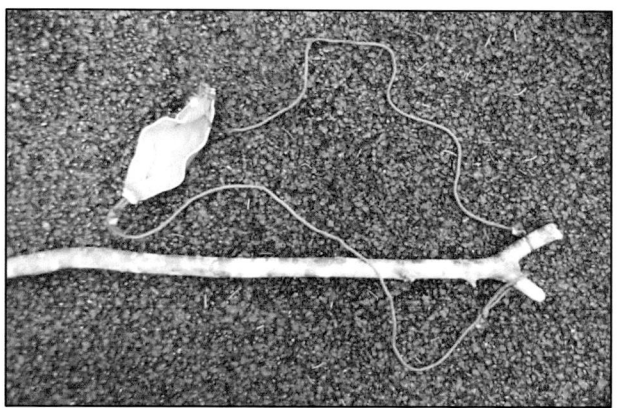

FIGURE 39. STAFF SLING.

The *initial* ammunition used was rounded pebbles in the range 55g-75g, which is within the range of those found on Iron Age sites – see Chapter 3. A selection of the stones is shown in Figure 40; for the trials they were painted red to facilitate retrieval. The six stones for each set of casts were held in a small bag, convenient for the slinger to load and cast them quickly.

FIGURE 40. SELECTION OF SLING-STONES.

As mentioned above, circumstances required a change of ammunition. Participant 2 and the later part of Participant 1's trials used red golf balls, weighing 45g. All subsequent trials, including those of Participants 1A-1D, used air-dried clay shot, also painted red. The shot were rolled by hand into rough spheres weighing between 55g and 68g, with a mean weight of 60.9g, standard deviation 3.7g.

Figure 41 shows the three types of ammunition in comparison. The clay shot in this photograph are 56g, 58g and 62g respectively (bottom row, left to right), the stones being 67g and 75g (top left and top right respectively) and the golf ball 45g.

FIGURE 41. COMPARISON OF AIR-DRIED CLAY (BOTTOM ROW) AND OTHER TYPES OF SHOT.

Target

An adapted golf practice net was used as a target. This was collapsible and light enough to move around the site fairly easily. It is shown in Figure 42.

The target provided three types of score:

- The central hanging section was the principal area that the slingers attempted to hit, and is roughly the size of a small person (width 86cm at the top and 38cm at the bottom, by 144cm high; total area 0.85m^2). Movement due to hits on it could be readily observed. In calm air it hung vertically; the bottom corners were restrained by elasticated cords to hold it in place on windy days.
- Within the inner target, a circular pocket backed by a net (diameter 29.5cm, area 683 cm^2) was represented to the slingers as a vulnerable area of the attacker, such as the head of an attacker otherwise protected by a shield.
- The net represented a group of attackers. Its maximum dimensions were 3.07m wide by 2.05m high, its total area being 5.10m^2. The area that the target presented was controlled by guying it to an approximately upright position, as shown in Figure 43.

FIGURE 42. TARGET (METRE RULE ON LEFT).

FIGURE 43. TARGET ON INNER FACE OF OUTER RAMPART, GUYED UPRIGHT.

Signals and Notices

Warning signs were placed around the area being used for the experiment, to prevent passers-by straying into the danger area. Further signs positioned at the four main access points to the hillfort forewarned visitors of the nature of the experiment. Exhibits of the signs may be found in Appendix A. A whistle was used to signal the start of each trial and to warn of the approach of passers-by or animals.

Procedure

The instructions to the participants are exhibited in Appendix A.

Each participant cast six stones in quick succession at each target position (when 'defending') or *from* each position (when 'attacking'). The experimenter signalled by whistle the start of each set of six stones and timed it, recording the result for each stone on a score sheet. After each set of casts, stones were collected, the target was moved to its next position (or the participant moved, in the 'attacking' case) and the procedure repeated. There was a break of a few minutes between the major conditions. Each participant also cast a few stones as practice and to warm up, allowing familiarisation with the target.

Safety and Ethics

A number of aspects of the experiment procedure derived from a risk analysis prepared according to the safety processes of the University of Winchester; see Appendix A for a summary of the analysis and associated plan. An Ethics Analysis was prepared and is also shown in the appendix.

The use of previously-experienced slingers was a key factor in the safety analysis, ensuring reasonable control over the stones. Safety points in the procedure were the use of whistles and notices to avoid endangering the public, and care when moving on steep sections of the ramparts. A first aid kit and emergency contact instructions were held on site, and the over-riding importance of safety was stressed to participants.

Results

The principal results of the experiment are reported below. Appendix B includes the full ('raw') scores, selected data gathered from the participants and tables with details of the performance analyses and analysis of variance.

The overall results are summarised in Figure 44, by participant. 'Hits' refers to stones hitting the inner part of the target representing an individual opponent and

Participant	Shots	Head Hits	Hits	Net Hits	Total Hits	%
1	144	11	34	57	91	63.2
1A	144	7	44	55	99	68.8
1B	144	10	44	63	107	74.3
1C	144	17	43	51	94	65.3
1D	144	10	44	57	101	70.1
2	144	1	17	49	66	45.8
3	60	0	0	4	4	6.7
4	84	1	5	20	25	29.8
5	84	1	1	9	10	11.9
6	84	1	1	15	16	19.0
7	102	0	9	20	29	28.4
Total	1278	59	242	400	642	50.2
Includes P1-1D	720	55	209	283	492	68.3

FIGURE 44. OVERALL SLINGING RESULTS BY PARTICIPANT.

includes 'Head Hits' on the circular inner net. 'Total Hits' is the sum of 'Hits' plus 'Net Hits' that impacted elsewhere on the net target, including its frame.

The table shows the number of shots for each participant - 144 shots represents four complete sessions (that is, attack and defend each of the ramparts). The participants' hit-rates varied significantly, and as not all the participants completed all sessions of the trials, this must be taken into account when comparing results across the conditions. For this reason, much of the comparative analysis uses the results only of Participants 1 to 1D and 2; in each case the set of participants contributing data is stated.

Qualitative Results and Observations

The main qualitative observations are described first, as some of them should be borne in mind when interpreting the later charts.

Approximate Accuracy and Range

Figure 44 shows that most participants missed the target more than half the time; the experimenter kept track of this by noting 'near misses' and shots that fell short of the target. These subjective observations were sufficient to form a judgement that the slingers were always roughly on target and that the short casts were due to problems of aiming, not to inadequate range. Exceptions were one 'wild' shot due to a mis-release and a few cases of the stone falling from the pouch before being cast. The conclusion about range is confirmed by some shots passing the target by more than 50m.

Downhill and Uphill Slinging

It was noted in the first trials of Participants 1 and 2 that no advantage due to height was apparent, comparing attack with defence. Subsequent participants took a few practice casts both uphill and downhill. This is discussed further in Chapter 6.

Slinging from Sloping Stances

The experiment required participants to sling from several positions on slopes (positions UA3, UA5, BA7 and BA9 in Figures 34 and 35). Several slingers commented that this was awkward, especially on the slopes of the main ditch. One slinger suggested that position BA7 (on the down-slope of the inner ditch) could be omitted, as 'no-one would ever stop to sling from there.' While his comment may be right, it was noted that he and others scored more hits *from* that position than they scored *against* that position from the level stance above, demonstrating the value of measurements to complement expert opinion.

Slinging Styles

Each slinger used his most practised style, even when it seemed inappropriate; attempts to switch styles reduced performance. It seems likely that Iron Age slingers would practice techniques appropriate to the distances and angles involved at the site.

The styles used were: 'Greek,' where the stone is brought from an aiming position in front of the slinger down through an arc in a vertical plane on his right and forward to a release point with the arm pointing towards the target; 'Figure 8,' where the stone is brought back on a curved path above the head then straight forward toward the target ('Ampersand' might be a more accurate name); 'Apache,' where the stone starts in a hanging position and is brought up behind the slinger and released above and forward of his head; 'Overhead,' where the stone is whirled in a horizontal plane above the head; and 'Underarm,' where the stone is whirled in a vertical plane, the forward-going part of its arc at the bottom.

These names were ascribed to the styles by the slingers; they acknowledged that 'Apache' is a misnomer. This style was sometimes reduced to a simple 'flip' of the stone from behind the slinger, producing a high lob rather than a direct trajectory toward the target; the Underarm technique also produced a high trajectory. As operated by these slingers, Overhead and Underarm involved several revolutions of the stone before release, the others only a single movement.

As each slinger adopted his preferred style, the effect of style on accuracy is inseparable from the individual slingers' skill; a great deal of time and training would be needed to make a valid comparison.

It appeared that the Underarm style was not suited to slinging from the ditch, although its high lobs were suited

FIGURE 45. SLING-STONE HOLES IN MEDIUM-DENSITY TARGET.

Abbreviation	Term	Meaning in the Experiment and Analysis
A, Att	Attack	
B, Bi	Bivallate	Related to the inner rampart in the experiment
BA1, BA2, etc.	Bivallate Attack	Positions the inner rampart was 'attacked' from
BD1, BD2, etc.	Bivallate Defend	Positions the inner rampart was 'defended' against
D, Def	Defend	
	Effectiveness	Probability of a Hit incapacitating its target
	Head Hits	Sling-stones striking the head-sized target pocket
	Hits	Sling-stones striking the inner, man-sized, target
	Net Hits	Sling-stones striking the outer part of the target
N. S.	Not Significant	Effects of this factor are not statistically significant
T1, T2, T3	Tactic 1, 2, 3	Attacking tactics, explained on page 66
	Total Hits	Sling-stones striking any part of the target
U, Uni	Univallate	Related to the outer rampart in the experiment
UA1, UA2, etc.	Univallate Attack	Positions the outer rampart was 'attacked' from
UD1, UD2, etc.	Univallate Defend	Positions the outer rampart was 'defended' against

FIGURE 46. TABLE OF ABBREVIATIONS USED IN RESULTS CHARTS.

to 'plunging fire' *into* the ditch or any lower target position; also, it would not work from immediately behind a parapet. The Greek and Figure 8 releases produced flatter trajectories and observably more forceful hits, but may have been less suited to downhill slinging.

Effectiveness of Hits

An informal trial demonstrated the effectiveness of hits by sling-stones. Figure 45 shows holes pierced through medium-density board hanging from the target frame, by stones of approximately 65g cast from about 10m.

The impact of sling-stones was also demonstrated by twelve holes through the net, by damage to the frame of the target and by stones being buried irretrievably in the ramparts.

Accuracy and Timing Results

Key to Abbreviations and Graphs of Results

Figure 46 gives a key to the abbreviations used in the charts and tables of experiment results below.

Figure 47 illustrates the symbols and line styles used in most of the graphs of results.

Summary Statistics

The accuracy results, shown by participant in Figure 44, are summarised by main condition in Figure 48. The table shows an advantage to attackers in the univallate case and much higher hit rates for the univallate case than for the bivallate case. (There are further details in the tables in Appendix B.)

Meaning	Symbol or Line Style	Example (1)	Example (2)
Attacker Scores	Dashed Lines		
Defender Scores	Solid Lines		
Univallate	Single Lines		
Bivallate	Double Lines		
Head Hit	Head icon		
Hit	Man icon		
Net or Total Hits	Group icon		

FIGURE 47. LEGEND FOR RESULTS CHARTS.

The overall hits data for all participants are shown by position in Figure 49. An increasing trend can be seen within each series (UA1-UA5, UD1-UD5, BA1-BA9 and BD1-BD9) as the distance to target decreases, and a generally higher hit rate in the univallate case.

	Condition	All Participants			Participant 1-1D		
		Uni	Bi	Total	Uni	Bi	Total
Hits	Attack	47.6	7.8	20.2	57.3	13.3	31.7
	Defence	33.8	8.8	17.5	42.7	14.8	26.4
	Total	40.7	8.3	18.9	50.0	14.0	29.0
Total Hits	Attack	85.7	31.6	48.5	96.0	51.4	70.0
	Defence	78.1	38.4	52.1	88.0	51.4	66.7
	Total	81.9	34.7	50.2	92.0	51.4	68.3

FIGURE 48. AVERAGE HIT RATES BY CONDITION (PERCENTAGES).

(Note that these results are not balanced for number of casts or participant skill.)

The two positions BA4 and BD4 are of note, as in these cases the slinger could not see the target – either he or the target was in the dead ground of the outer ditch. When attacking from this position only one net hit was scored, but while defending against it 17 total hits were registered. That case apart, the attacking scores are slightly higher than defending scores.

Although the timing data is incomplete due to damage to the stopwatch, in Figure 50 a clear distinction can be seen between the times of Participants 1, 1A-1D and 2 on the one hand and Participants 3-7 on the other. This may be due to practice and perhaps slinging style; the first group were more certain in placing the stone in the pouch and rotated the sling only once.

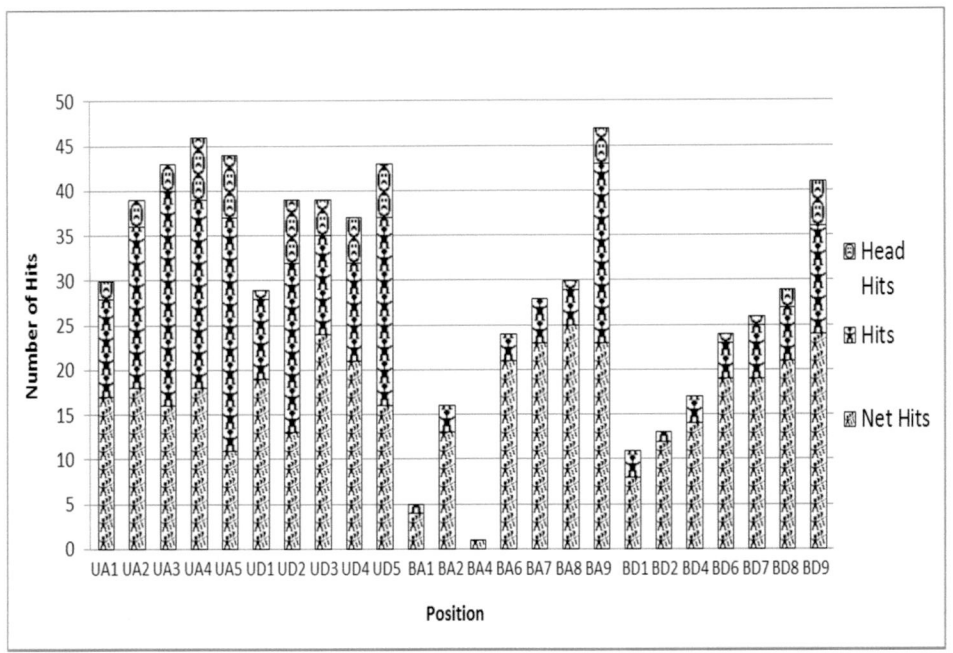

Figure 49. Overall Hits by Position, All Participants.

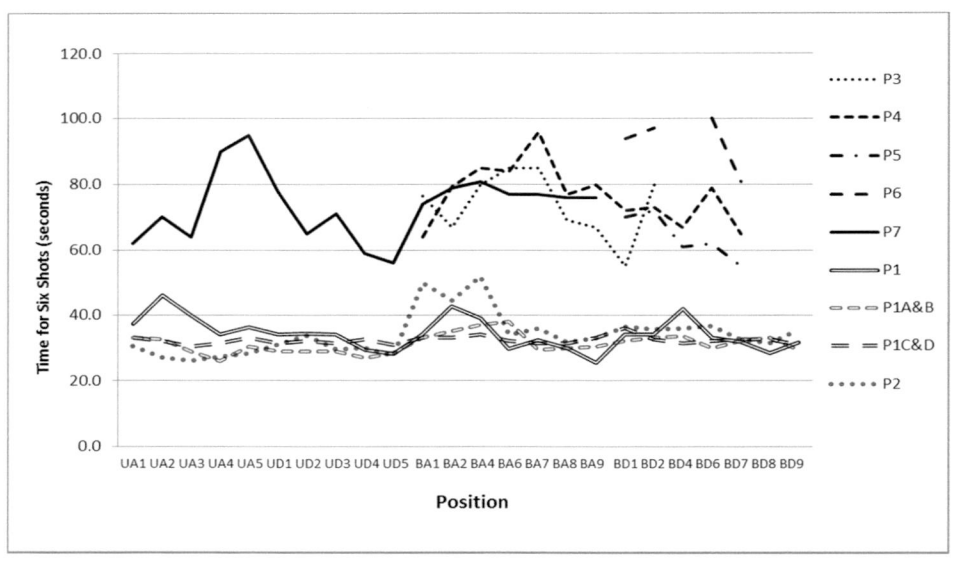

Figure 50. Time for Six Casts, by Participant and Position.

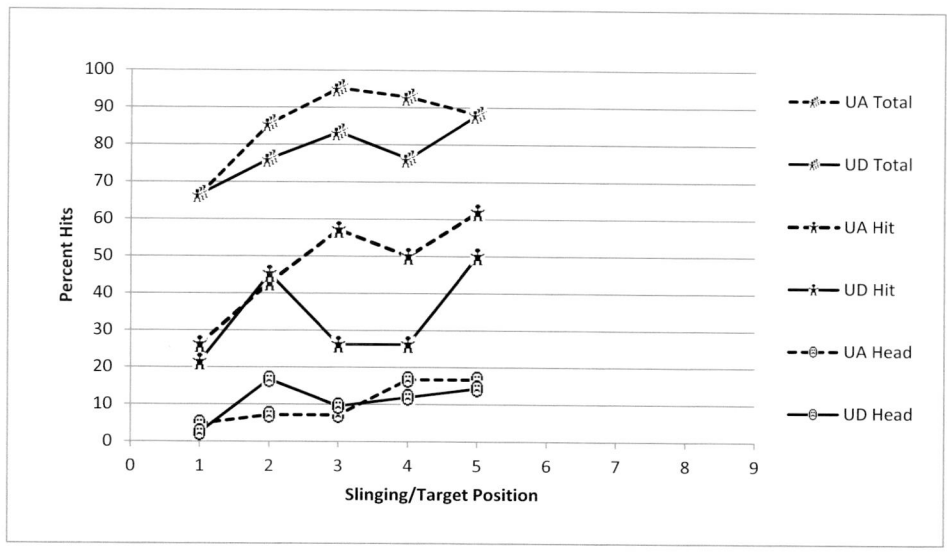

FIGURE 51. UNIVALLATE HIT RATES, ALL PARTICIPANTS.

Attack Versus Defence

The hit-rates for all participants are shown in Figures 51 and 52 for the univallate and bivallate cases, respectively.

Figure 51 shows an advantage to the attackers, due to a dip in the defenders' accuracy ('UD Hit') for Positions 3 and 4 when the target was on the outer slope and bottom of the ditch, which may be a downhill-slinging artefact.

Figure 52 is less clear because of the lower rates generally, but the *defenders* appear to have the advantage in this case.

In the analysis of variance, Attack/Defence comparisons were not found to be statistically significant, except for the Total Hits measure in one case (see 'Analysis of Variance' below).

Univallate Versus Bivallate

The higher hit rate in the univallate case can also be seen in the data from Participant 1's five sessions, shown below. The dip in 'UD Hits' shown in Figure 53 causes much of the defensive disadvantage, and could be an effect of his 'Figure 8' style when slinging downhill.

Figure 54 shows the lack of hits from the outer ditch in the bivallate case (Position 4).

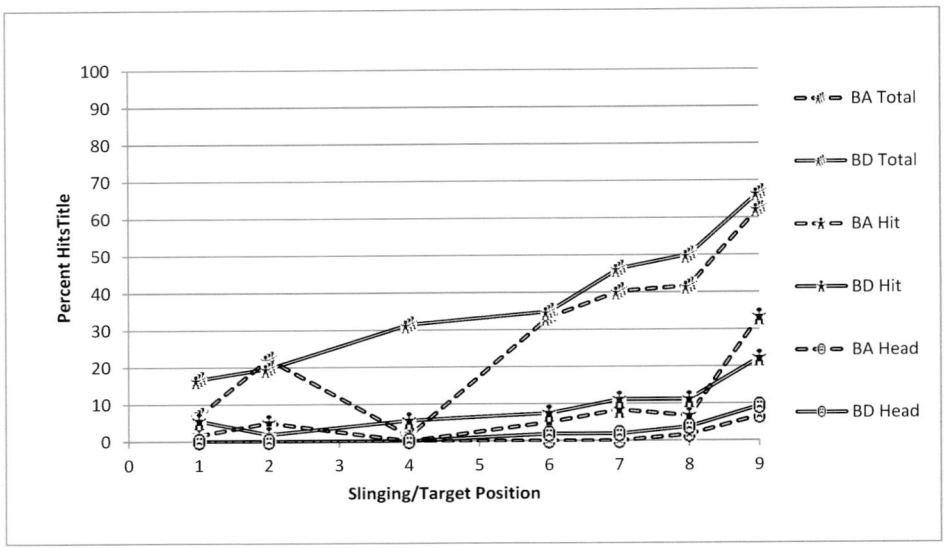

FIGURE 52. BIVALLATE HIT RATES, ALL PARTICIPANTS.

The analysis of variance showed that the rampart-type and position effects were statistically significant.

Distance to Target

The hit rate graphs in Figures 51 to 54 are plotted against positions, which are comparable across the conditions but not evenly spaced; Figures 55 to 57 include distance to target.

Figure 55 shows probability of hitting the inner target, plotted against distance to target, for all participants. A downward trend with increasing distance is evident, despite the dip in 'UD Hits' in the outer ditch. The trend is more marked in Figure 56, which shows 'Total Hits.'

Finally, the hits versus distance graph for Participant 1-1D, Figure 57, again shows the strong relationship between probability of hit and distance to target and also the low score when attacking from the dead ground of the outer ditch (at about 37m).

Correlations

Across all participants, the negative correlation between hit probability and distance to target was -0.93 for Total Hits and -0.79 for Hits. The values for Participant 1-1D were -0.92 and -0.80, respectively.

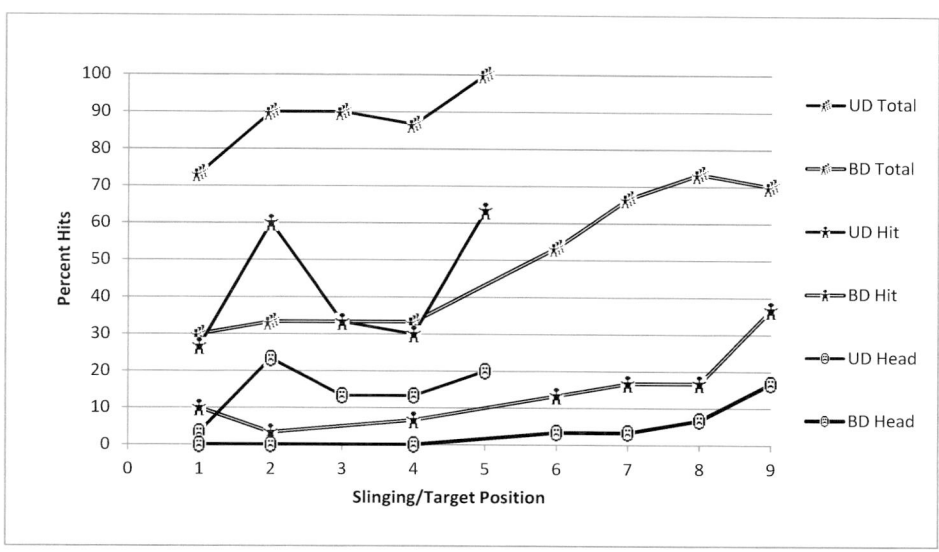

FIGURE 53. DEFENDING HIT RATES, PARTICIPANT 1-1D.

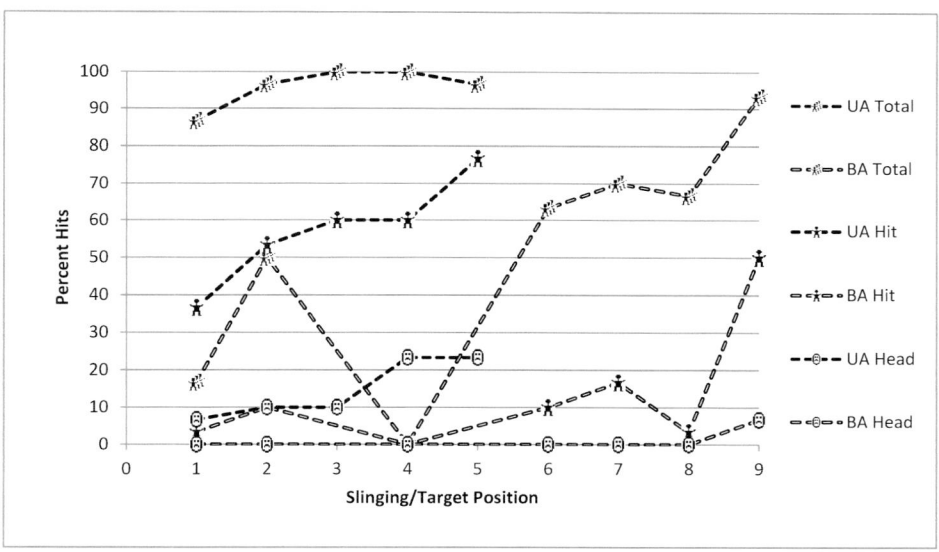

FIGURE 54. ATTACKING HIT RATES, PARTICIPANT 1-1D.

The time taken for a set of six casts was positively correlated with distance to target (0.73 for all participants and 0.67 for Participant 1-1D) and negatively correlated with hit-rate (-0.78 and -0.64 for Total Hits and Hits respectively, for all participants.) A simple interpretation of this is that more difficult shots take longer.

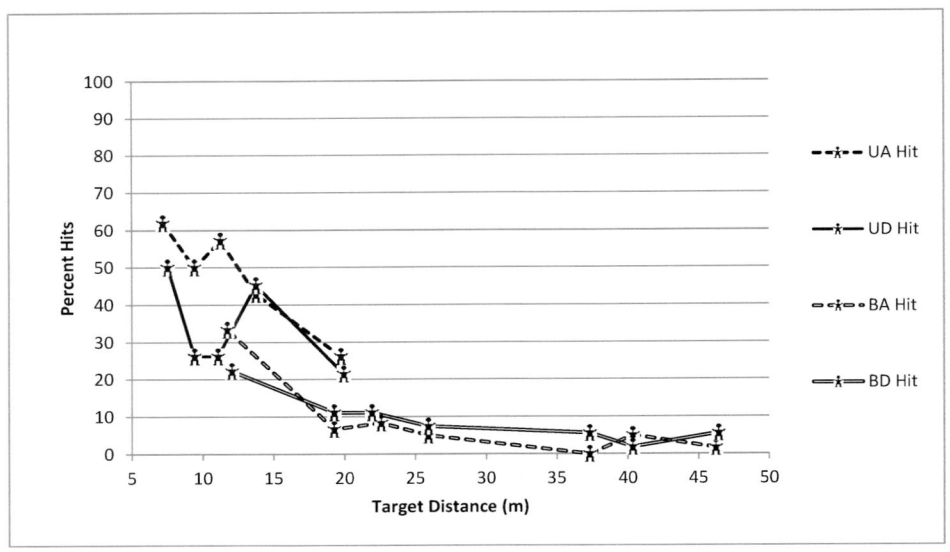

FIGURE 55. PROBABILITY OF HIT ON INNER TARGET VERSUS DISTANCE, ALL PARTICIPANTS.

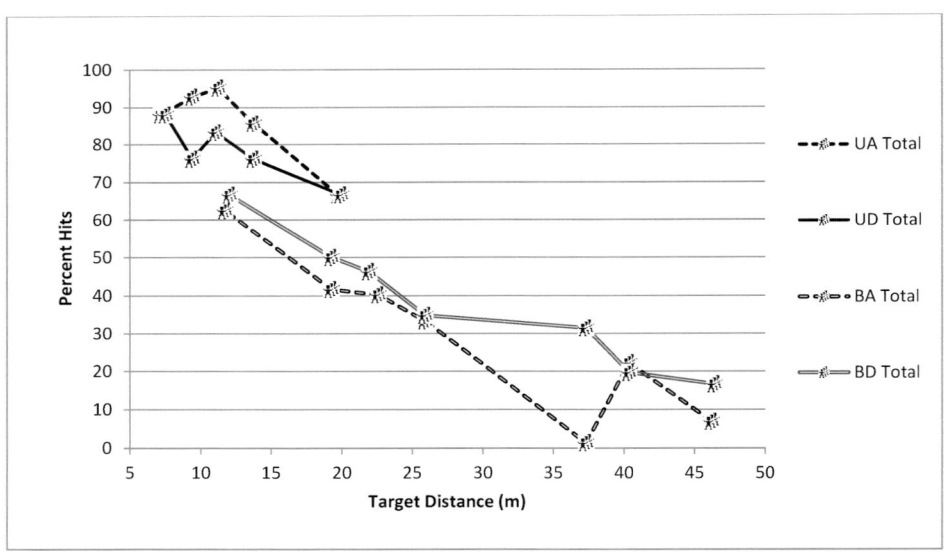

FIGURE 56. PROBABILITY OF TOTAL HITS VERSUS DISTANCE, ALL PARTICIPANTS.

Analysis of Variance

The accuracy data were subjected to multivariate analyses of variance (ANOVA) using the IBM Statistical Package for the Social Sciences 19 (SPSS). Full details

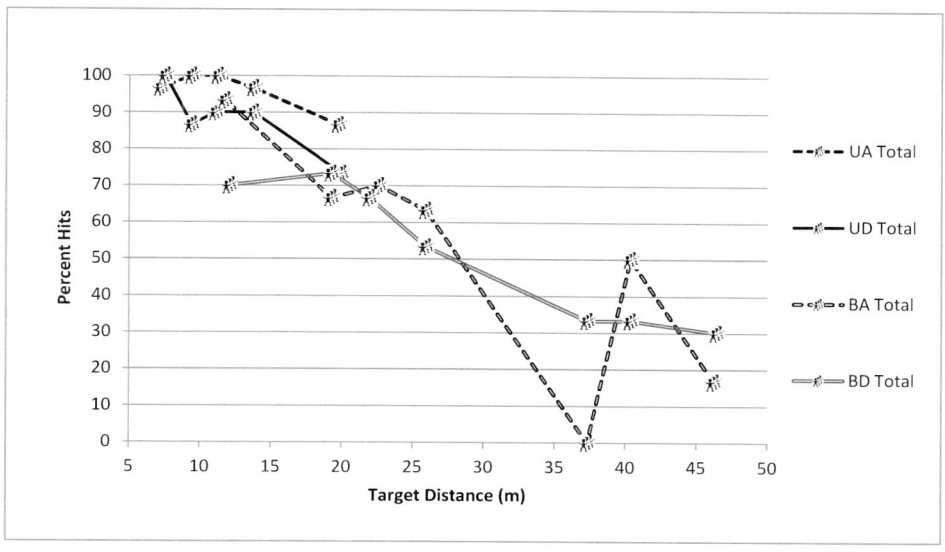

FIGURE 57. PROBABILITY OF TOTAL HITS VERSUS DISTANCE, PARTICIPANT 1-1D.

of the analysis, including formal statements of significance findings and the SPSS summary tables, are given in Appendix B.

To take advantage of the repeated measures design, the analysis chosen was the General Linear Model Repeated Measures option as described by Gray and Kinnear (2012: 336-346). The analysis compared Hits and Total Hits for the 'position,' 'rampart-type' and 'attack/defend' factors. This analysis requires data collected from subjects who experienced all the conditions, and therefore only data from Participants 1-1D and 2 were used. A further requirement is for equal numbers of levels within the factors compared, requiring subsets of the data to be selected. Two sets of positions were considered to be comparable, and a separate analysis was conducted for each.

The first set analysed was Positions 1, 2 and 4 for both ramparts, because their location 'on the ground' was the same in the two cases. The second set analysed was Positions 2, 3, 4 and 5 of the univallate case against Positions 6, 7, 8 and 9 of the bivallate case: these are comparable positions relative to the defenders. See Figure 35 for illustrations of the positions.

The statistical significance results are summarised in Figure 58; omitted interactions were not significant on either measure.

Although the statistical significance results provide reassurance that the experiment was sensitive enough to detect effects from the main factors, there is

	Hits Measure					
	Same on Ground			Relative to Defenders		
	df	F	p	df	F	p
Rampart Type	1, 5	71.49	< .001	1, 5	37.50	.002
Position			N. S.	3, 15	12.11	< .001
Attack/Defend			N. S.			N. S.
A/D x Rampart			N. S.			N. S.
Rampart x Position	2, 10	4.52	.040			N. S.
	Total Hits Measure					
	Same on Ground			Relative to Defenders		
	df	F	p	df	F	p
Rampart Type	1, 5	110.00	< .001	1, 5	32.22	.020
Position	2, 10	6.69	.014			N.S.
Attack/Defend			N. S.	1, 5	11.35	.020
A/D x Rampart	1, 5	10.25	.024			N. S.
Rampart x Position			N. S.			N. S.

FIGURE 58. STATISTICAL SIGNIFICANCE SUMMARY FROM ANOVA.

little in these results that cannot be explained by the effects of distance to target and of the dead ground in the outer ditch.

Effective Range

An informal trial was conducted on 'effective range,' meaning the range at which a slinger could engage a target, rather than the maximum distance he could reach.

Thirty-six shots were aimed at the target horizontally along the main ditch of the hillfort, from between 40m and 70m away, after the slinger had already cast 330 shots for score and about 40 practice casts that day. Figure 85 in Appendix B shows full details of the results. The shots were observed from the main rampart and all were below the observer, on a relatively flat trajectory less than 5m above the level of the slinger's feet; far from the 45° maximum-range trajectory. All except one were close to the target. These results show that effective range is more than 70m, even after a day's slinging.

Time Required to Assault the Defences

A further informal trial established approximate timing for a simple assault on the defences. Two volunteers ran from outside the hillfort to the top of the outer and inner ramparts respectively, along the slinging lines of the experiment. The 'assaults' were repeated twice and recorded on video. Frame-by-frame analysis of the video was used to construct a timeline, indicating the minimum time an attacker would be exposed in each section of the defences. There was a further 'validation run' with two student volunteers, on the ramparts of Cadbury hillfort in Devon.

The timeline was used as the 'Basic' speed in the Tactical Analysis, the overall assault time being 18.0 seconds for the outer rampart and 37.5 seconds for the bivallate case. These are the times during which the attacker was exposed to defensive slinging – from 75m outside the hillfort to about 2m below the rampart top, where hand-to-hand combat would commence. Variations of these times for different attacking tactics and speeds are shown in Figure 59.

Tactical Analysis

This analysis uses data from the experiment to examine tactics and aspects of the design of the defences, mostly assuming equal numbers of equally-skilled slingers on each side. The accuracy data show that attackers and defenders had similar hit rates and that the advantage varied by position. However, they do not reflect the tactical situation; to explore this further, other factors must be taken into account:

- The objectives of the attackers and defenders; put simply, the attackers' objective is to get into the hillfort, and the defenders' is to keep them out.
- Timing of shots; different positions had different slinging rates (Figure 50).
- The time required for attackers to approach through the defences (measured in the informal trial).
- Effectiveness: the likelihood that a hit incapacitates an opponent.
- The effect of being under attack, on slinging rate and accuracy (and the benefit of 'covering fire').
- The effect of shields, parapets, or other protection.
- The effect of the differences between the hillfort in its Iron Age condition and its condition during the experiment.

Where the experiment provides data on these factors, they have been combined with the accuracy results in the tactical model. The other factors are not dealt with mathematically, but are discussed qualitatively.

The first scenario is described in some detail, to establish the assumptions; for later scenarios the focus is mainly on the results.

Scenario 1: Direct Assault by Small Group of Attackers

In this scenario, a small number of attackers approach the hillfort quickly and attempt to cross the defences directly to a point where they can engage the defenders hand-to-hand. An equal number of defenders opposes them with slings.

The number of hits achieved by an attacker is calculated from the probability of a hit in each position, found in the experiment, times the number of shots from that position determined by the attacker's tactics. The number of hits achieved by a defender is calculated from the hits per unit time measured in the experiment for each target position, combined with the time that the attacker would be in that area, from the assault time trial. Additionally, the exposure time is increased by 6 seconds for each shot the attacker takes. (This allows a fraction of a second for the attacker to pause and prepare for slinging.) The attackers are assumed to be in effective range at 75m from the outer rampart.

The model includes three speeds of attack: 'Basic,' based on the informal trial; 'Fast' which represents a fitter or more practised attacker; and 'Slow' which allows for attackers carrying shields and weapons or the slopes being more slippery than during the trials.

Three attacking tactics are analysed: 'Slinging,' 'Intermittent Slinging' and 'No Slinging' (Tactics 1, 2 and 3, or 'T1, T2, T3' respectively). In Tactic 1, the attacker stops to sling one stone from each of the positions. In 'No Slinging,' the attacker does not pause to cast stones, but attempts to get to hand-to-hand distance as quickly as possible. In 'Intermittent Slinging,' the attacker slings stones from the level stances and when close – three in the univallate case and four in the bivallate case.

The times to make an assault without pausing to sling, at the three speeds, and the number of shots per attacker for the three tactics, are shown in Figure 59.[3]

The numbers of hits predicted by the model are shown in Figure 60.

Figure 60 shows the number of hits by each attacker and by each defender ('A' and 'D' respectively). It shows that the advantage is always with the defenders

	Time of Assault (seconds)			Attacker Shots		
	Basic	Fast	Slow	T1	T2	T3
UA	18.0	12.5	21.5	5	3	0
UD	18.0	12.5	21.5	5	3	0
BA	37.5	27.3	45.5	7	4	0
BD	37.5	27.3	45.5	7	4	0

FIGURE 59. TIMING AND ATTACKING SHOTS FOR SCENARIO 1.

Rampart	A/D	Basic			Fast			Slow		
		T1	T2	T3	T1	T2	T3	T1	T2	T3
Univallate	A	2.9	1.9	0.0	2.9	1.9	0.0	2.9	1.9	0.0
Univallate	D	3.8	3.1	1.3	3.4	2.7	0.9	4.1	3.4	1.6
Bivallate	A	0.9	0.7	0.0	0.9	0.7	0.0	0.9	0.7	0.0
Bivallate	D	2.6	2.2	1.4	2.2	1.8	1.0	2.8	2.5	1.7

FIGURE 60. INDIVIDUAL HITS FOR SCENARIO 1.

---

[3] The total time of an assault depends on both running speed and the number of times an attacker stops to use the sling. For example, at six seconds per shot, a Basic-speed attack on the outer rampart using Tactic 2 would take 36 seconds (18 + 6x3). The longest, a Slow-speed attack on the inner rampart using Tactic 1, would take 87.5 seconds (45.5 + 6x7). See also Figure 81 in Appendix B.

Speed	Basic			Fast			Slow		
Tactic	T1	T2	T3	T1	T2	T3	T1	T2	T3
D/A Ratio									
Univallate	1.3	1.6	∞	1.2	1.4	∞	1.4	1.8	∞
Bi	2.7	3.0	∞	2.4	2.5	∞	3.0	3.4	∞
D-A Difference									
Univallate	0.9	1.2	1.3	0.6	0.8	0.9	1.2	1.5	1.6
Bi	1.6	1.5	1.4	1.3	1.1	1.0	1.9	1.7	1.7

FIGURE 61. DEFENSIVE ADVANTAGE, SHOWN AS RATIO AND DIFFERENCE IN HITS PER MAN, FOR SCENARIO 1.

despite the hit-rates reported above. It also confirms that faster is always better from the attackers' point of view.

Note that the repeated values in these tables are correct: the hits by attackers depend on the number of shots dictated by the tactic, which is the same at different speeds, and the speed of assault is the same for both attacking and defending hits.

Considering the different tactics, it appears that an attacker making a quick direct assault could expect to be hit once even if 'fast,' but that there is surprisingly little difference – 10% of a hit – in his average vulnerability between the univallate and bivallate cases for Tactic 3. More generally, although the defenders' performance is lower in the bivallate case compared to the univallate, the attackers' performance is even more reduced.

Figure 61 shows the advantage to the defenders both as a ratio (defensive hits over attacking hits) and as a difference (defensive hits minus attacking hits). From the ratio part of the table, it appears that 'bivallation' roughly doubles the defenders' advantage. The difference part shows that the improvement is between 0.1 and 0.7 of a hit per opponent. This again suggests that the best choice for attackers would be to move quickly; in a more protracted engagement, the 'force multiplier' effect shown by the ratio view would be more likely to prevail.

The results above are per individual for hits on the inner target – the 'man.' A similar analysis for a of group six attackers against six defenders, using the 'Net Hits' data from the experiment, showed that an individual in a close group could expect

Rampart	A/D	Basic			Fast			Slow		
		T1	T2	T3	T1	T2	T3	T1	T2	T3
Univallate	A	3.3	2.1	0.0	3.3	2.1	0.0	3.3	2.1	0.0
Univallate	D	4.7	3.7	1.6	4.2	3.3	1.1	5.0	4.1	2.0
Bi	A	1.5	1.1	0.0	1.5	1.1	0.0	1.5	1.1	0.0
Bi	D	3.6	3.0	1.8	3.5	2.9	1.6	3.9	3.4	2.2

FIGURE 62. HITS PER INDIVIDUAL IN GROUPED ATTACK AND DEFENCE.

additional hits due to near misses of stones aimed at his comrades. The results are shown in Figure 62; note that this shows hits per individual, assuming equal groups of six attackers and defenders (the inner target was one sixth of the area of the net).

The implications of this are that slingers should keep widely-spaced. The defenders, however, are somewhat restricted by the width of the rampart. The attackers have also to consider concentrating their forces to make a breach at a point in the defences. Each side's tactic will depend on how many attackers and defenders are in the vicinity and on responding to the other's choice of tactic. A small group should spread over a few metres; the tactics of larger groups are discussed in Scenario 2.

Probability of Being Hit during an Assault

An alternative model computed the *probability* that a given attacker would suffer or achieve a hit. This showed that an attacker has little chance of reaching the defenders without being hit. For example, an attacker using Tactic 1 at Basic speed has a 4% chance of reaching close-combat distance on the inner rampart of the bivallate hillfort without first being hit by a stone.

His likelihood of getting there without being *stopped*, however, would also depend on the *effectiveness* of the hits. Figure 63 illustrates a selected subset of cases. At 100% effectiveness, a slow-moving attacker has little chance

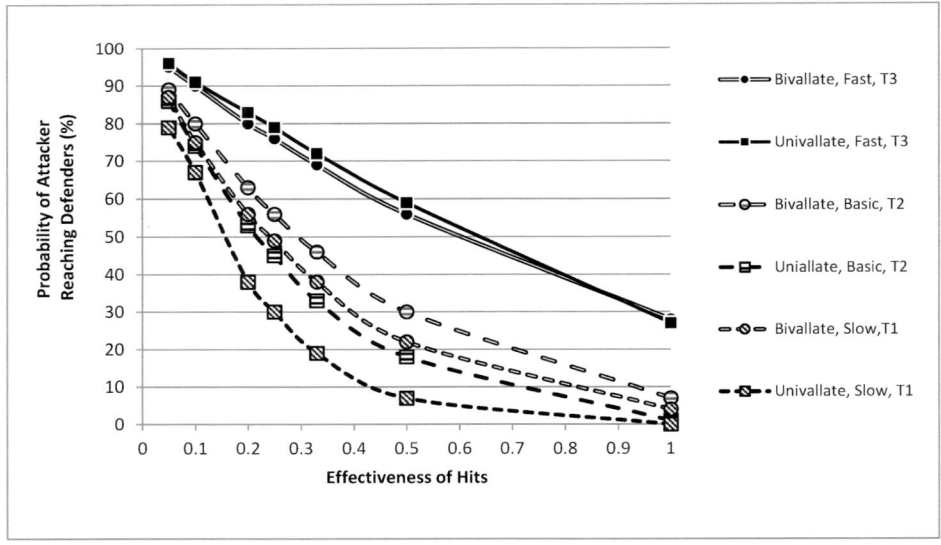

FIGURE 63. PROBABILITY OF ATTACKER REACHING HAND-TO-HAND COMBAT FOR THREE SPEED-TACTIC COMBINATIONS (DEFENSIVE STRENGTH CONSTANT).

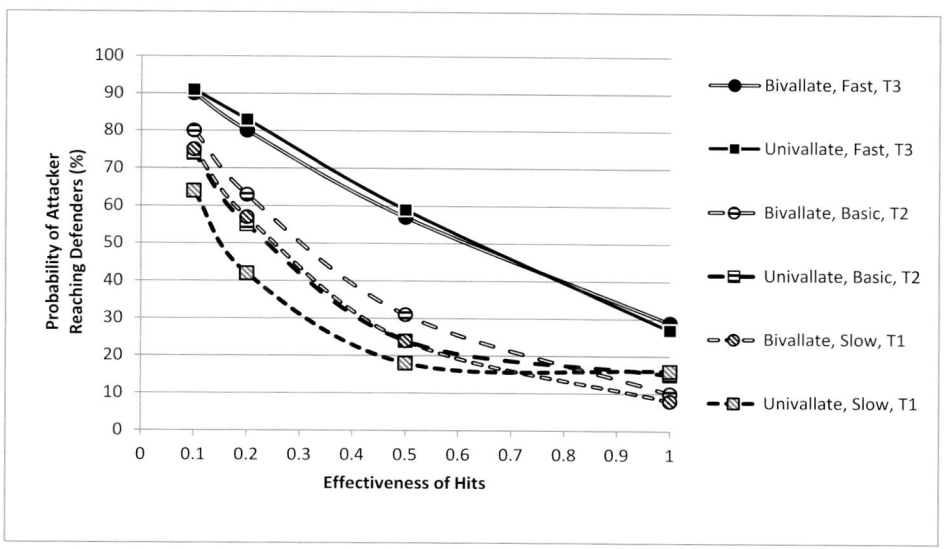

FIGURE 64. PROBABILITY OF ATTACKER REACHING HAND-TO-HAND COMBAT DISTANCE FOR THREE SPEED-TACTIC COMBINATIONS, INCLUDING EFFECT OF ATTACKING SHOTS.

of reaching either rampart, but if effectiveness is reduced, for example by a shield, then his chances improve significantly. Effectiveness of 1 means every hit stops its target, 0.5 means half the hits stop their target, and so on.

These calculations used the direct Hits data and assume constant numbers on each side; they are comparable with Figure 61. The assumption of constant numbers implies that fresh attackers and defenders move from elsewhere to a critical point in the defences as the battle proceeds. However, if no such reinforcements were available, the above results are biased because they take no account of hits *by* the attackers. This is corrected in Figures 64 and 65.

Speed	Tactic	Effectiveness			
		1	0.5	0.2	0.1
Univallate					
Basic	T1	16	23	50	70
	T2	15	24	55	74
	T3	20	51	78	89
Fast	T1	17	25	52	72
	T2	15	27	58	76
	T3	27	59	83	91
Slow	T1	16	18	42	64
	T2	15	24	54	74
	T3	14	44	74	86
Bivallate					
Basic	T1	9	25	58	76
	T2	10	31	63	80
	T3	19	45	74	86
Fast	T1	10	31	63	80
	T2	14	39	70	84
	T3	29	57	80	90
Slow	T1	8	24	57	75
	T2	9	29	61	78
	T3	18	43	72	85

FIGURE 65. PROBABILITY OF ATTACKER REACHING HAND-TO-HAND COMBAT FOR SELECTED SLINGING EFFECTIVENESS VALUES.

The Tactic 3 results do not change, as there are no attacking shots to account for, but this last adjustment indicates improvement in the attackers' chances with Tactics 1 and 2. The levelling-out of the curves at higher effectiveness is due to all the defenders being eliminated (starting at six per side).

Other Factors

A number of other factors must be considered when assessing the tactics associated with Scenario 1, that go beyond the data generated by the experiment and that have therefore not been included in the numerical analysis.

Moving targets. The attackers rely on their speed to get them through to the point where they can engage the defenders hand-to-hand. This movement would make them harder to hit; that is, the defenders' hit-rate would reduce. This factor therefore favours the attackers and also increases the advantage of Tactic 3 (and of Tactic 2 over Tactic 1).

Choosing when to sling. The defenders might respond to the above by choosing their moment. Slinging when the attacker is slowest or least able to move unpredictably would reduce the defenders' rate of slinging but produce a better hit-rate. Against a mass attack this would not be necessary. With practice, the defenders' range for particular points on the defences would become very accurate.

Slinging while running, or stopping to sling. The assumption built in to the timing figures, that an attacker can sling a single stone in six seconds, is optimistic if accuracy is to be maintained. Some of the slingers consider, however, that they could learn this skill. Allowing only a fraction of a second penalty is probably a bias in favour of the attackers in Scenario 1.

Effect of suppressing shots. No allowance has been made for the effect on either side of 'covering fire' by the other, because its value is unknown. It is assumed to have similar effect on both sides.

Defensive aids. No direct correction for shields or parapets has been included, but this can be regarded as part of the effectiveness-of-hits factor. (For example, if every hit on the body is incapacitating but three quarters of hits are on the shield, the effectiveness would be 0.25.)

Scenario 2: Barrage from the Edge of the Defences

In this scenario, the attackers arrive at the outer edge of the defences and proceed to bombard the defenders, who sling back at them. The model proceeds in rounds of shots at equal speeds by both sides. The 'Hits' data for Positions 1 and 2 (just outside the defences and on the counterscarp bank) were used to predict attrition of the two sides, with a further variable for effectiveness of hits – the probability of a hit incapacitating the opponent to the extent that he ceases slinging.

Figure 66 shows how many rounds of slinging are required until one side wins ('Rounds'), and how many slingers the winning side has left at that point ('End'). A group of slingers was deemed to have lost if their number fell below 0.5 of a slinger ('x').

The first two rows of Figure 66 show that starting with equal groups of six attackers and six defenders and an effectiveness of 0.5, for the univallate case the attackers win at the ninth round of slinging (about 45 seconds), but have themselves only one man left standing at that point. Changing the balance by adding just one defender (rows 5 and 6) meant that the defenders win at the sixth round (30 seconds), with three men left.

The six-versus-six situation for the bivallate case (rows 3 and 4) produced a stalemate – both sides had two men left after 33 rounds and one left after 50 rounds. Favouring either side with an additional slinger stopped the contest at 34 or 35 rounds, with that side having four men still slinging.

Observations from Figure 66 include:

1. Equal numbers favours the attackers in the univallate case.
2. Equal numbers produces stalemate in the bivallate case.

Rampart	Att/Defd	Start	Effectiveness 0.5 End	Rounds	0.33 End	Rounds	0.25 End	Rounds	0.2 End	Rounds	0.10 End	Rounds	0.05 End	Rounds	Note
Uni	A	6	1	9	1	13	1	17	1	22	1	44	2	50	1
	D	6	x		x		x		x		x		2		
Bi	A	6	1	50	2	50	<3	50	3	50	4	50	5	50	2
	D	6	1		2		<3		3		4		5		
Uni	A	6	x	6	x	9	x	11	x	14	x	28	1	50	3
	D	7	3		3		3		3		3		3		
Bi	A	6	x	35	x	52	<2	50	2	50	4	50	5	50	3
	D	7	4		<4		4		4		5		6		
Uni	A	12	10	3	10	4	10	5	10	6	10	12	10	23	4
	D	6	x		x		x		x		x		x		
Bi	A	12	10	16	10	23	10	31	10	38	>10	50	11	50	4
	D	6	x		x		x		x		2		4		

FIGURE 66. RESULTS OF BARRAGES.

3. Adding a single defender changes the result in the defenders' favour in the univallate case but stalemate persists in the bivallate case, unless effectiveness is more than 0.33.
4. A 12:6 numerical advantage for the attackers means that they win quickly in the univallate case but still need 16 or more rounds of slinging in the bivallate case, opening up the possibility of reinforcements.

The table shows that reducing effectiveness draws out the contest without changing its ultimate conclusion, whereas increased outnumbering brings a quicker conclusion. The model was limited to 50 rounds of slinging as the uncertainties in the data preclude identifying a winner in a closely-balanced case.

Figure 67 shows selected cases from this analysis. Note that the bivallate results (double lines) are the same for attackers and defenders and the univallate results (single lines) are all lower than the equivalent bivallate results. In the univallate cases, the defender results (triangle markers) are lower than the equivalent attacker results (round markers). This shows that bivallate cases tend to stalemate and that univallate defenders are at a disadvantage, but of less than one man in six.

Defensive Reinforcements

The attackers would concentrate forces at a single weakly-defended point in the defences, to produce numerical superiority there. If the bombardment goes well for them, they have the option to change tactics: when the defending force is

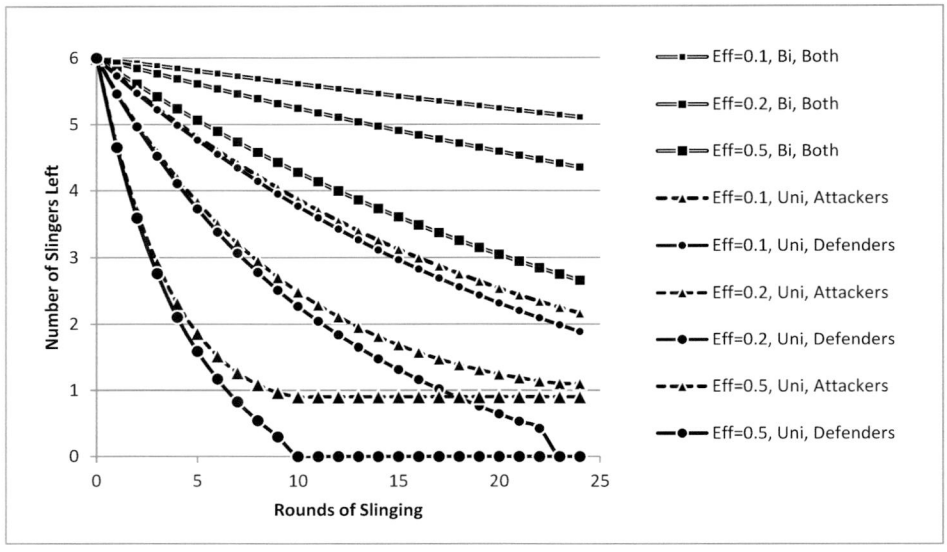

FIGURE 67. NUMBERS OF ATTACKERS OR DEFENDERS LEFT STANDING FOR 24 ROUNDS OF SLINGING, FOR THREE LEVELS OF EFFECTIVENESS.

destroyed or severely weakened, they can switch to a direct assault with relative impunity. At the same time, the defenders would call for assistance if they were outnumbered at a particular location. The outcome, then, would depend on whether defensive reinforcements arrive before the attackers have had time to gain a foothold on the rampart.

A direct assault against little or no defensive slinging would take between 4 and 8 seconds from the counterscarp to the outer rampart but between 19 and 33 seconds to the inner rampart. Considering Figure 67 and given that a round of slinging takes about five seconds, it appears that in the univallate case a superior force of attackers can clear the outer rampart and establish themselves on it in between 30 seconds and a minute, which may be too little time for the defenders to reinforce it. In the bivallate case, on the other hand, the two-to-one force would need two or three minutes for this, and would be vulnerable to shots from defenders on either side while scaling the rampart.

To explore this, the model was modified to include defensive reinforcements of six slingers at intervals of 15, 30 and 60 seconds. These could represent slingers already on the rampart moving to the point of action, slingers in reserve from the interior, and slingers being brought from elsewhere on the defences, respectively.

In the bivallate case all these reinforcements are sufficient to protect the rampart even from a 12:6 superiority of attackers; in the univallate case, the 30s and 60s reinforcements do not succeed in protecting the rampart unless effectiveness is low. (For details, see Figure 89 in Appendix B.)

Slinging Effectiveness

Up to this point in the tactical analysis, the effectiveness of the slinging has been assumed to be the same for both sides; a 'Hit' by a defender would be as likely to cause injury as a 'Hit' by an attacker. However, this would not necessarily be the case. In addition to statistical variations, two potential systematic differences are the slinging skill levels of the two forces and the presence of greater protection for one group than the other.

Based on Finney's (2006) work, in Chapter 4 it was suggested that the ultimate defence of the hillfort would involve all members of the community, including women, youths and older men. On the other hand, a moderate-sized group of attackers would be composed mainly of warriors. Even if the defenders were skilled slingers, the *force* with which they used the weapon would therefore likely be less than that of the attackers, making the effectiveness of hits less (ignoring the counter argument that warriors would disdain the use of the sling, as a weapon suited to women and children).

Protection reducing the effectiveness of a sling-stone hit could come in the form of shields, armour including helmets, and parapets on the defences. Given the composition of forces just described, shields were more likely deployed by the attackers and of course parapets would protect the defenders. Within this part of the analysis, both these mechanisms are considered to be included in effectiveness.

Scenario 3: Two-Stage Assault and Defence of Bivallate Defences

This scenario examines whether the defenders of a bivallate hillfort would benefit from defending the outer rampart first, retiring to the inner rampart if necessary, and if so what the tactics of the two sides might be if the attackers gain a foothold on the outer rampart.

In the initial defence of the outer rampart, defenders on the inner rampart could sling against approaching attackers over the heads of their comrades on the outer rampart. This would not be safe, however, once attackers reached the defences.

In these tactical analyses, the slinging phase of the battle is over if the attackers reach the rampart. This does not necessarily mean that the overall outcome is in the attackers' favour; defending warriors on the rampart still have the advantage of height in hand-to-hand combat. However, the bombardment scenario showed that a skilful group of attackers might clear the defenders from a section of the outer rampart in a minute or so, unless reinforcements arrived rapidly. A fast-moving group of attackers who concentrated their forces at a weakly-defended point might therefore achieve a foothold on the outer rampart.

Once established on the outer rampart, the attackers appear to have three options (excluding retreat): they could directly assault the inner rampart, they could resume bombardment of the inner rampart, or they could move along the outer rampart to another point in the defences.

The first of these is a continuation of Scenario 1: the attackers would continue to be at a disadvantage, especially as already weakened while taking the outer rampart, and would therefore need a significant advantage in numbers or effectiveness to succeed. If this were the only breach of the outer defences, defenders would concentrate in the area. The attackers would also be vulnerable to slinging from defenders to either side of them on the outer rampart, reducing the value of shields as the stones would come from several directions. (This could be a reason for defenders to move onto the outer rampart should a breach occur.)

The second option is a closer-in version of Scenario 2. The model was therefore modified, with the attackers starting from the outer rampart. From there, they need 14 to 20 seconds to reach an undefended point on the inner rampart. With equal force sizes and slinging effectiveness, the attackers are all disabled in about 20 rounds of slinging (less than two minutes). To clear the inner rampart of defenders for the 20 seconds required to scale it, they need a 15:6 superiority of numbers over the defenders and high effectiveness, if the reinforcement rate is 30 seconds.

The third option, proceeding along the rampart, would only make sense if a position of advantage was close, as the attackers would suffer from slinging from the inner rampart and perhaps from ahead and behind. Even with shields their attrition rate would be high relative to their effect on defenders. Two positions of advantage could be: first, to join with attackers at another breach of the defences nearby, concentrating forces; and second, if the outer rampart provided a position from which to assault the hillfort entrance.

In conclusion, the defenders would generally be best to defend from the inner rampart, assuming the initial position of their forces allowed it, especially as this maintains their flexibility to move to critical points in the defences. An exception might be the case of very large defences, such as Maiden Castle, where the intermediate ramparts could be defended and greater numbers of defenders might be available. It appears that attackers reaching the outer rampart should continue the direct assault, rather than try to 'sling it out' from there.

Assaults on Entrances

The experiment did not trial slinging at the entrance of the hillfort, but the hit rates for given heights and distances can be extrapolated to the positions of defenders and attackers on and below the banks comprising hillfort entrances.

Three cases are considered below: a simple in-turned univallate entrance, as shown in Figure 9; a developed entrance of modest complexity, based on that at the Steepleton Gate of Hod Hill, Figure 11; and a more complex developed entrance based on that at Danebury, Figure 11, or Crickley Hill, Figure 68.

In the simple case, having reached the causeway leading to the entrance the attackers would have to transit about 20m under fire from defenders on the ramparts either side and perhaps on a bridge above the gate. Unless they have achieved surprise or have distracted the defence through diversionary tactics, they can expect to receive not only heavy barrages of sling-stones, but spear-thrusts, hand-thrown stones and perhaps hand-to-hand opposition in the passageway or through the gate. The amount of time required to reach the gate if unopposed would only be a few seconds, but longer would be required to destroy the gate, especially by fire. During this period they would be constrained to a small area and difficult for defending slingers to miss.

The tactical advantages gained by the more elaborate entrances include time: if the attackers have numerical superiority at the entrance, a longer passage or a second gate provides time for the defenders to move forces into play. The Hod Hill case involved a corridor of around 90m for the attackers to transit before reaching the gate – more than four times that of simple cases such as The Trundle. The other defensive advantage is that attackers would be vulnerable to slinging from several directions, including from behind, which would be much more difficult to shield against. With small numbers of defenders slinging against them, the Scenario 1 results show that they can expect several hits each while in this area (Figure 62). Once defensive reinforcements arrive, the Scenario 2 results predict that they would survive a few minutes at most, even with shields (Figure 66).

At Danebury or Crickley Hill (Figure 68), getting past the outer gate would lead the attackers into a killing zone of the defenders' choosing, any delay at the inner gate providing time for slingers to gather around and above them. Unless the attackers contrive to outnumber the defenders in the area of the gates by barrage or surprise they would be likely to fail with heavy losses.

Surprise or Diversionary Tactics

Most of this analysis has assumed comparable forces on either side of the action. However, if one side outnumbers the other with similar effectiveness, then the larger force wins the slinging phase, especially if defending; the attackers could therefore benefit from surprise. This would be most easily achieved by a small fast-moving group of raiders, although what such a group would be likely to achieve is not obvious.

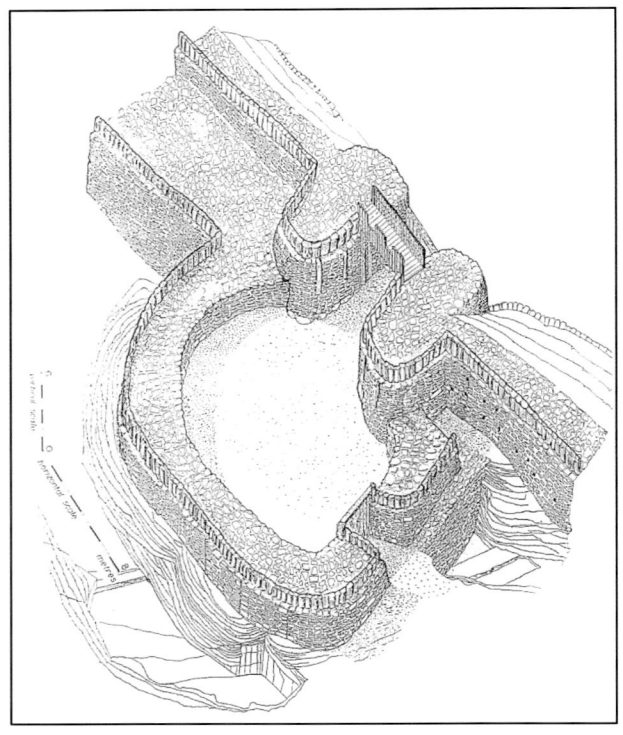

FIGURE 68. PHASE 3B ENTRANCE AT CRICKLEY HILL (FROM DIXON 1994, ILL. 185; BY KIND PERMISSION OF PHILIP DIXON).

Chapter 6: Discussion

This chapter first reviews points arising from the discussion of hillfort function in Chapter 2. It then discusses issues and caveats associated with the experiment and the tactical analysis, before going on to consider tactical issues beyond the scope of the experiment.

Functions of Hillforts and Hillfort Defences

It was established in Chapter 2 that hillforts and hillfort defences are not the same thing and that characteristics of the defences are independent of variations in the interior features.

Defensive Features and Characteristics

Hillfort defences have characteristics that are shared with defensive structures from most parts of the world throughout history, such as ancient and medieval walled cities, pre-Inca hilltop fortresses, Napoleonic forts and Maori *pā*. They are usually sited to use the terrain to advantage; they present a steep face and other obstacles to the outsider, place insiders at a height advantage, hide the dispositions of the interior, and limit access through entrances which themselves share these features.

Some low-lying Iron Age sites have similar enclosing works and are classified as hillforts despite their location; as discussed in Chapter 2, the presence of defences is the key identifier of hillforts. Although without steep approaches, these sites – such as Cherbury – often had defence provided by water, making them less anomalous than might first appear (Harding 2012).

A particular difficulty for the proponents of non-defensive interpretations is to explain the specific features and size of the defences. Symbolic structures could take many forms (towers, pyramids and cursuses come to mind) and the community-building benefits of their construction would be much the same whatever their shape. Why, then, did the British Iron Age produce thousands of hillfort defences, and so few other large structures?

One response to that question it is to challenge the defensive interpretation on its own terms: to suggest that the structures were not suitable for defence, or went beyond what defence requires. The unsuitability of choice of *site* for military purposes is also argued as part of this case, including overlooked sites and sites with poor internal visibility.

In the hillforts literature, 'defence' is often taken to imply a 'military' function for the whole hillfort. However, if one distinguishes the function of the hillfort from that of its enclosing works, it becomes apparent that there is no contradiction in the idea that a site might be chosen for non-defensive reasons, independent of the decision to defend it with ramparts and ditches. Thus 'defence' takes on its narrower literal meaning: it is about protecting the site and its contents, not about building a military base. Some sites being less than perfect militarily does not preclude defence being the function of their enclosing works.

Even from a military perspective, the importance of these issues is questionable; sites such as Scratchbury and Hod Hill being overlooked (Bowden and McOmish 1989) is not necessarily significant and in the latter case could only be avoided by not building the hillfort. Maiden Castle, Swaledale (Figure 69), is more difficult to explain: its southern rampart is overlooked by the hillside, but could have been built a few metres further up, avoiding this problem. Bowden and Blood (2004) suggested it is 'not a hillfort,' implying that the rampart is purely a boundary, but not explaining its size or position.

Hill-slope sites chosen for intervisibility with their associated territory, as at Scratchbury, may even have had defensive benefits that outweigh the overlooking disadvantage, in terms of lookouts, warning and signalling.

FIGURE 69. SOUTHERN DEFENCES OF MAIDEN CASTLE, SWALEDALE.

Regarding other criticisms of the practicability of the defences, one again notes the paucity of detail in the analysis. Maiden Castle (Dorset) may appear too large for defence by slingers and to include dead ground where attackers could shelter (Bowden and McOmish 1987), but Wheeler (1943: 48-51) drew different conclusions from the same information. Finney (2006: 80) suggested that many ditches and banks did not add to defence: '*clearly, there is another rationale behind multivallation*,' while stating elsewhere that multivallate defences protected against the range of his sling. The results of the present experiment showed the tactical value of larger defences and put a different perspective on the dead ground.

Evidence of Other Functions

Excavation of hillforts provides evidence for many functions, varying over time and place, which have been suggested as alternatives to defence. However, these are functions of the hillfort interior; to test whether they explain the defences, one must ask if they would require to be surrounded by large banks and ditches. While recognising that they might vary, '*there may be no such thing as a typical hillfort,*' Cunliffe (2006: 154) provides a convenient summary of the probable functions of hillforts. Paraphrased, it includes: defence in time of unrest, enclosure for communal pastoral activity, defined space for social or religious interactions, settlement (permanent, cyclic or elite), storage for communal surplus, focus for redistribution and production, and territorial marker.

What do these functions require from the hillfort defences? The first, 'defence in time of unrest' obviously refers to the defences, and implies that what is being defended is the *people* of the community.

The next two functions – enclosure for pastoral activity and defined space for special activities – would require some level of enclosure, as needed for controlling stock, marking a boundary and perhaps hiding the interior from view and casual access. They might explain the small 'defences' of the Earliest Iron Age sites but would not require the large structures and complications of the Middle and Late Iron Age.

Settlement is shown by the evidence of houses and domestic activity, and might require boundaries for practical reasons and social reasons such as privacy, but would not use large ramparts and ditches except for defence. The functions of storage and focus for redistribution likewise: these require practical and visible boundaries, and some level of security from theft, but would not need large ramparts around the whole site.

The last of Cunliffe's functions – territorial marker – would only require the line to be visible, not insurmountable.

Thus, the large structures of the Middle and Late Iron Age go well beyond what is needed for practical hillfort functions apart from defence. The interior functions might, however, define *what* was being defended – the people of the local community, their houses and possessions, their food storage and their religious sites. The strategic value of stored food resources (Cunliffe 2005: 427) could be particularly important.

This leaves three non-utilitarian functions to be discussed: that the defences were boundaries, that they symbolised the prestige of the community, or that the social benefits of the construction process were what mattered most. Of course, these functions would have occurred together: but that would be an unavoidable *effect* (or side-effect) of having the defences, whatever the primary purpose in building them.

It is clear that the defences form a boundary around the hillfort interior, and that boundaries were, and are, important to people. However this does not explain their size or the specifics of their features; there are many Iron Age boundaries and enclosures of much more modest proportions than hillfort defences (Collis 1996; Cunliffe 2005: 589; Sharples 2010: 120).

The defences would be important to people living within and near them, giving them meaning that went beyond the merely practical; the defences separated the internal space from the rest of the world and entering that space may have had special significance. The special deposits found in boundary structures, particularly ditches, are argued to show the symbolic nature of the defences (Bowden and McOmish 1987; Hill 1995; Hill 1996). However, while these confirm the *importance* of the barrier, they do not demonstrate its function. The evidence from sites like South Lodge or Little Woodbury (Bowden and McOmish 1987) that a boundary ditch might be dug, deposits made and then the ditch back-filled or allowed to silt may show that those boundaries were established symbolically, but hillfort enclosures were enlarged and maintained and are still physical barriers two millennia later.

The defences would have impressed anyone who saw them and could be seen therefore as symbols of power and prestige, whether of the community, of its chieftain, or of some special class. This overlaps the 'defensive' rationale – a visitor, even from another hillfort, would get the message of deterrent capability. This argument relies on the defences being complete – there may be weaker or stronger points, but a facade without continuation to its sides and rear would be both defensively useless and unimpressive. In some cases, however, presenting an impressive facade to approaching visitors would result from putting the strongest defences toward the likely, or constrained, direction of approach of enemies.

As reported above, the community-building and emotional benefits of constructing the defences have been proposed as their main purpose (Lock 2011; Sharples 2010: 296). While the number of hillforts and their survival value may imply that positive emotions were involved, direct evidence is absent; resentment of coercion, slavery, injury and wasted resource might equally feature. Further, other constructions could achieve community-building effects, but were made only in very small numbers; the White Horse (Miles *et al*. 2003) might be one example.

Authors' Perspectives and Consensus

Both sides of the discussion accuse the other of making interpretations based on their own mind-set – Heath (2009: 118) refers to them as 'hawks and doves' - it is inevitable that one's experience and personality play a part in forming judgements. However, it is a weak argument to suggest that a military assessment is invalid because it was made by General Pitt Rivers or Brigadier Wheeler, just as it is to accuse others of wishful thinking; only arguments based on the evidence of the archaeology are persuasive.

Although the discussion is described as two opposed schools of thought, all the authors accept that a single answer is inadequate to cover the whole period and that hillforts had multiple functions: there must be the '*possibility of alternative and multiple understandings*' (Lock 2007: 346). Although defence is the only function that explains the features of the surrounding works, they would also have had effects as boundaries, as symbols and on community cohesion.

The Experiment and Analysis

The experiment appears to be unique in providing measurements, especially on accuracy, from the use of slings at a hillfort. It is not surprising, therefore, that a number of methodological developments and lessons resulted; however, the main point of discussion is whether the results of the experiment fill any of the identified gaps in knowledge.

Interpreting the Data

From the first look at the results from Participants 1 and 2, it was apparent that some assumptions had to be put aside, as the expected advantage of height for the defenders was not evident in the data; in fact the attackers scored more hits. This appeared to be due to the unfamiliarity, for modern slingers, of slinging downhill but raises the question of whether this is simply unrepresentative of the Iron Age or whether the advantage of height is illusory.

A little reflection produced the answer 'both.' Iron Age defenders might be assumed to practice and become highly accurate on their own ground, and the attackers could hone their required skills also. The advantage of height is mainly in extending *range*; once the contest was within range for both sides, there is no accuracy advantage for either. The defensive hit rate might have been higher in the Iron Age, but the evidence of the trials is that distance to target, not height, is what matters.

This does not mean that building defences was wasted effort. Putting the data into a tactical context produced a rather different outcome: in the univallate case the contest remained fairly even, but in the bivallate case a significant advantage for the defenders appeared (Figures 60 and 61). For equal numbers and skill levels, attackers were at a disadvantage of up to 3:1 in terms of hits and with moderate slinging effectiveness were unlikely to reach hand-to-hand combat with defenders on the inner rampart. Only by bringing to bear greater numbers or greater skill could they expect to reach the interior.

Before concluding that this demonstrates Avery's hypothesis, however, one must look at validity of the data. There are three main issues: the reliability of the data, the degree to which the measurements and scenarios represent Iron Age circumstances, and the excluded factors that might be important.

The Tactical Analysis relies on hit rates from the experiment; these are the best data available. However, for representing tactical outcomes, they are only estimates. The data show distance to target being the over-riding factor for accuracy, as indicated in 'Results' above.

That being the case, and given that defending scores were low due to unfamiliarity with downhill slinging (especially Participant 1-1D against positions UD3 and UD4), then the tactical analyses here are probably biased against the defenders. For example, the need in Scenario 2 for there to be seven defenders to defeat six attackers in the univallate case (see Figure 66) is probably due to experimental artefact rather than underlying attacking advantage.

This shows that the exact numbers in the accuracy results above should not be taken too literally, although they provide a basis for statistical comparisons within the experiment, as shown by the ANOVA results.

Having noted that caveat, some more-general observations can be made. Firstly, the importance of distance to target means that the bivallate case is very different from the univallate, once attackers reach the defences. Secondly, time is also an important factor: the period of exposure of the attackers while scaling larger defences puts them at a great disadvantage, as shown for the bivallate case in Scenarios 1 and 2 and as suggested for developed entrances in 'Assaults on Entrances' above.

Chapter 6: Discussion

Representativeness of the Iron Age

The main weakness of the experiment as a 'predictor' of Iron Age tactics and outcomes lies in the areas where the experiment conditions were not representative of those in the Iron Age. There may be unknown elements to this, but issues are evident with the slingers and their performance, with the modern state of the hillfort defences, and with the limitations of the experimental paradigm.

The most practised of the participants was the most convincing as a sling warrior. The high variability in hit rate between participants suggests that a regular user of the sling for hunting or herding who also practiced at the site could exceed the performance even of Participant 1, especially if slinging style were better adapted to the downhill cases.

The ramparts are currently covered in ridged turf and may be a little lower than in the Iron Age, but are within the range described on page 36. The main topographical issues are the depth of the ditch and the outer face of the 'univallate' rampart.

Examination of the section of the northern defences (Richmond 1968, figure 65) shows that the main ditch was just over 2m deeper when cut than in the 1950s – see Figure 17. Additionally, it was much steeper – especially the drop from the outer rampart. Relative to the experiment, therefore, an Iron Age attacker would have required two or three extra seconds to cross this ditch, would have been at greater risk of a fall and would risk being trapped within the ditch. If the slopes were maintained as chalk or scree, as suggested at Danebury (Cunliffe 2005: 355), even more time would be needed. Iron Age footwear might also have been less suited to fast assault times than the volunteers' boots. These differences mean that the experimental bivallate analyses are significantly biased in favour of the attackers.

Considering the outer rampart as representing the univallate case, the main issues are that the ditch is rather shallow and there is no wooden or stone face to the bank. The overall height to be scaled, at about 4.3m, is at the lower end of the range described by Avery (see page 36); the estimate for Hod Hill is 6.1m (Richmond 1968: 10). The experiment therefore again favours the attackers, but note that the model stops where the attackers reach hand-to-hand combat, which could be at the base of a low, faced section. Such facing is assumed to have been rough enough for attackers to scale it if unopposed, as in parts of Scenario 2, but again may have required more time.

Hod Hill today lacks parapets, although there is evidence for them in the Iron Age. Richmond's reconstruction (Figure 16) includes a breastwork on the main rampart about 0.9m high on its inner side. In this, the experiment is again biased in favour of the attackers: the parapet would have shielded the defenders, reducing attackers' slinging effectiveness by perhaps a third (as well as protecting defenders from spear thrusts in the close combat phase).

The effect of shields, helmets and other armour is likely to have been more mixed. If as suggested above, the defence was 'all hands' but the attack was primarily by warriors, the latter would be likely to be better-protected. On the other hand, carrying this equipment would slow down a direct assault and would interfere with attackers' slinging. In a contested barrage (Scenario 2) shields would reduce defensive slinging effectiveness by, say, a half, but also reduce the attackers' slinging *rate* by a similar degree.

The final set of representativeness issues is related to the fact that the experiment did not simulate combat conditions – there was no return fire, covering fire, movement while slinging, slinging at moving targets, or interference from other weapons and tactics. Without further evidence, it can only be surmised that these would reduce the rate and effectiveness of slinging, possibly in favour of the moving attackers. The associated motivational effects might be significant, but could go either way and would vary by individual and circumstances.

In summary, a number of issues prevent the experiment being realistically representative of the Iron Age. This does not mean that the results are false, but that they are indications and insights rather than accurate predictions. The factors considered suggest that the tactical analysis is significantly biased in favour of the attackers, compared to Iron Age conditions.

Further Tactical Considerations

The experiment and tactical analysis are based on limited tactics and small numbers of combatants within a small area of action, and assumes that the numbers can be multiplied up as necessary (that is, thirty attackers facing thirty defenders produces the same outcome as six versus six). It is limited to the period between the attackers coming into range and them reaching hand-to-hand combat with defenders. Surprise and diversionary tactics were considered only as far as they would affect the numbers present at the point of action: the tactical model assumes that the attackers start outside the hillfort and that they are detected as they approach. This implies sentries or a warning system in the surrounding area, at least in times of insecurity, and that guards prevent enemies from entering the hillfort before hostilities commence.

Not all the defenders needed to line the rampart: familiarity with the defences would enable slinging from defenders safely behind it. (Participant 1 was able reliably to drop shots into the outer ditch from behind the inner rampart.)

The combination of Scenarios 1 and 2, some attackers assaulting the rampart while others applied a barrage, was not modelled quantitatively because no values are known for the effects of suppressing fire in these circumstances. The tactic may suit a particular mix of attackers, but there is no particular reason to assume that it would be successful. If it were, it would be on the basis that the barrage inhibited defenders' slinging enough to increase the chances of fast attackers reaching the rampart. However, offensive slinging would then have to stop, so a large barrage would be required to establish a bridgehead, and the defenders could shelter until the slinging paused.

Three further tactics are mentioned by Caesar in relevant contexts: the British use of chariots, the use fascines of brushwood to aid crossing ditches, and the use of large numbers of men to surround and bombard a hillfort.

As chariots and horses could not be used to scale defences, their influence on hillfort combat would be limited to the effect of timing – they were used as transport to and from the fighting (Harding 2012: 235) and might bring attacking forces in quickly, although the position of many hillforts would make even this difficult. Chariot battles beyond the defences are outside the scope of this study.

Although unsuccessful against the Romans (Rivet 1971), the Celts' use of fascines to aid crossing defensive ditches implies that they could have been employed at British hillforts. This might help to cross a small ditch, especially if missile defence was suppressed. Filling the main ditch of a developed hillfort, however, would be impractical against defensive slinging. (At Hod Hill at least 200 cubic metres of material would be needed, for a limited gain.) More realistically this tactic might deal with the steep bottom part of the ramparts, mentioned on page 83.

The Belgae tactic from Bibrax (see page 34) implies large armies and full-scale war, which may only relate to the Roman period. However, even though the walls there were '*denuded of men*,' the attack failed to breach the defences and was later driven off, by Balearic slingers amongst others (*De Bello Gallico*, II, 6). This is further evidence that defenders with slings had the upper hand unless facing superior forces.

The feasibility of defending the entire circuit of a hillfort has been questioned (Jennifer Foster, personal communication). Looking at a large site, one's impression is that it would be impossible to cover all of it, but if there were enough people to build the ramparts, perhaps there would be enough to defend them. Bibrax suggests that such a defence was possible, accepting that hillforts in Britain were different from first-century Gaulish *oppida*.

A rough estimate diminishes this problem. The circuit of Hod Hill is about 2km; a population of 300 adults and youths could place a slinger every 10m around it, plus 50 at the gates, with 50 more to rush to wherever the attackers concentrated. Skills and weapons beyond slinging would be required only by the latter group. This deployment could provide defence against a raid by similar numbers of attackers.[4] This size of population is plausible: based on Richmond's observations (1968: 8) and the geophysics results (Stewart 2006; 2008, Papworth 2011: 114), the hillfort could have had over 200 houses, though not simultaneously, and defenders could also be drawn from the surrounding area. It is within the ranges suggested by the rough population estimating methods described by Cunliffe (1984b: 560).

If defence was the purpose of the enclosing works, the absence of smaller, more-strongly defended internal structures in hillforts is puzzling: why is there no equivalent to a medieval castle keep? Garn Bodruan (Hillfort Study Group 2005) is the one possible exception visited during this study. Again, this suggests that raiding was expected, rather than full-scale or siege warfare.

The importance of the exposure time of attackers means other obstacles also fit the sling defence explanation. *Chevaux-de-frise*, slopes maintained as slippery or scree, low outer palisades, steep ditches and perhaps even the open ground of widely-spaced multivallation (as shown in Figure 8) would provide time for defenders to gather and bombard the attackers.

The relationship between outer ramparts and entrance complexes might provide an opportunity for analysis, in respect of both attacking and defending tactics. In Scenario 3, it was suggested that attackers might find that a foothold on the outer rampart was a better position from which to assault the entrance, and alternatively it could provide a route for defenders to be introduced onto the rampart or for defenders to retreat from outer ramparts, as Bowden and McOmish (1987) suggested was required. Inspection of a number of developed entrances makes this appear plausible; however, a meaningful analysis would require examination of the details of the rampart/entrance junctions for given phases shown by excavation, and would be a substantial investigation itself.

The Nature of Iron Age Warfare

The present tactical analysis examines the role of hillfort defences assuming that conflict took place there, using slings; it says little about the general form of warfare. However it does indicate that developed hillfort defences were suited to protecting against raids, and as the presence of hillfort defences was the primary

---

[4] Pitt Rivers' estimate of the 'garrison' of Cissbury being 5000 was based on very different 'modern notions' (Lane Fox 1869: 49)!

evidence for 'endemic warfare,' this supports the suggestion that raiding was the prevalent form of warfare (Cunliffe 2005: 541). Further, the lack of water-supplies made hillforts unsuited to defend prolonged sieges (Armit 2007).

If raiding was the main threat and was as frequent as the effort put into hillfort defences implies, then protecting resources (especially food stocks) in increasingly strongly-defended sites would have improved survival chances at the community level. The present study provides no new information with which to test this as an 'evolutionary' model (Dawson 1999; 2001), but it does raise the question of how community resources outside the hillfort, especially people and livestock, would be protected. Presumably, people close enough would shelter in the hillfort, and cattle would be hidden in woodland or dispersed to reduce losses. Lookouts and warning systems would be important, and intervisibility between the hillfort and its fields could be significant, as suggested by hill-slope sites.

Chapter 7: Conclusions

The discussion of the functions of hillforts and of their enclosing works may never be concluded: an activity involving perhaps the majority of the population over nearly a millennium will inevitably involve complexity and contradictions that cannot be fully resolved to the satisfaction of all, given the diversity of approaches to the question. A number of issues limit the conclusiveness of the present analysis; it relies on simple models built largely on data from one good slinger, and on incompletely represented Iron Age conditions. However, within those limitations the results do support Avery's suggestions regarding the development of Iron Age hillfort defences.

The experiment has provided measurements of the accuracy of slings in this context for the first time, as well as identifying a number of factors pertinent to the understanding of sling warfare. The tactical analysis based on the slinging results shows that there is defensive value in large ramparts, because of the time factors, and that developed hillforts would have regained the defensive advantage lost if sling attack was introduced against univallate defences. The critiques of the defensive capability of hillforts based on range, dead ground, heights and lengths of defences appear to have underestimated the tactical capabilities of the sling.

The insight that the hillfort defences would have functions separate from those of the interior is useful in clarifying some of the debate; the choice of site could be independent of the decision to defend it.

The enclosing works did form boundaries; their construction and maintenance would certainly affect community relationships, and what started as defences could over time have become symbolic. However, defence remains the most plausible explanation for the systematic development of structures whose size and form provide protection against the most common weapon of the Iron Age.

Appendix A: Procedure Exhibits and Experiment Equipment

The following pages show the forms, instructions and record sheets used in the experiment.

The pages show, respectively:

- Introductory Participant Instructions
- Safety and Environment Briefing
- Participant Instructions (for immediately before slinging)
- Data Record sheet
- Participant Details Record Sheets (2)
- Advanced (Site-entrance) Notice
- Warning Notice
- Emergency Instructions.

Participant Instructions – Introduction

Hillfort Defence Experiment – Outline and Instructions

Thank you for volunteering for the Hillfort Defence Experiment. This sheet gives you a summary of what you will be doing during the day and how you can help us get the best data from the experiment.

1. You will start with a briefing on how to ensure your safety and that of the other people around, and also how to ensure that we do not damage this ancient monument or the environment.
2. Then the experimenter will ask you for some details, such as how long you have been using a sling, how tall you are, and so on. All these details will be treated in confidence. No-one will be able to identify you or your data from the report.
3. You will have a few practice casts to warm up, get used to the target and make sure that it is clear how the experiment operates.
4. Then you will do four sessions of slinging, with breaks in between. You will cast six stones at a target, in each of five or seven positions – thirty or forty-two casts per session.
    a. In two sessions you will be 'defending' – you will stand on the rampart and the target will be moved toward you in five or seven steps, starting outside the ditch and ending up on the slope just below you.
    b. In two sessions you will be 'attacking' – the target will be on the rampart and you will cast at it from the same five or seven positions, moving closer each time.
    c. The order in which you attack or defend, and which of the two ramparts is used first, is different for each slinger, to 'balance' the experiment. The experimenter will tell you where to stand each time.
5. In every case, **try to be as accurate as possible**. The more hits on the target, the better.
6. The experimenter will be timing you. Make your six casts quickly, without pausing in between, but **do not sacrifice accuracy for speed**.
7. At the end of the experiment, you will be asked for your opinion on various aspects of it, and for any comments you wish to make.

If you have any questions, please ask.

If anything seems unsafe, at any time, then stop slinging and point it out.

Safety and Environment Briefing to Participants

Safety and Environment Briefing

Your safety and that of other people at the site is the priority: if at any time you have a doubt that what you are doing is safe, then stop and point out the problem to the experimenter.

In particular, please:

- Watch out for anyone being in the area where your stones might land (or any animal)
- Make sure you have a good stance as you cast (some cases are on slopes)
- Take care as you move across the ramparts – use an indirect route where it is easier, and use the trekking pole on the slopes.
- Take a few warm-up casts, and when slinging, don't try so hard that you strain something.

If you do hurt yourself in any way, or feel unwell, tell the experimenter straight away.

There is a small first aid kit and information on emergency contacts, in the Rucsac.

Please also take care of the ancient monument that we are operating on. In particular, try to avoid eroding the slopes.

If there is anything that seems unsafe, at any time, then stop slinging and point it out.

Participant Slinging Instructions

> ### Hillfort Defence Experiment – Slinging Instructions
>
> Now you have had some practice casts, here's how we will proceed:
>
> 1. The target: aim for the blue part of the target hanging in the middle – hit that as many times as you can. Any hit within the net is also good, and a hit in the pocket even better.
> 2. In every case, **try to be as accurate as possible**. The more hits on the target, the better.
> 3. The experimenter will be timing you. Make your six casts quickly, without pausing in between, but **do not sacrifice accuracy for speed**.
> 4. The experimenter will give a single long blast on the whistle, to warn anyone in the area that slinging is in progress; check there is no-one in the immediate vicinity.
> 5. When you are ready, a single short blast on the whistle means "start slinging".
> 6. When you have made the six casts, the experimenter will sound the whistle twice, to signal "all clear".
> 7. If you can say where each stone went, it will help in the scoring and in finding stones that miss. For example, say "a hit" or "net" for hits and "over" or "missed right" et cetera for misses.
>
> If you have any questions, please ask.
>
> **If anything seems unsafe, at any time, then stop slinging and point it out.**

Data Record Sheet

Date	P No	Expt Order	Safety Brief	P Details	Comments

Session 1: Rampart: _____ Attack/Defence: _____ .

Distance	Hits	Net	Miss	Short	U/K	Check	Time	Note
1								
2								
3								
4								
5								
6								
7								

Session 2: Rampart: _____ Attack/Defence: _____ .

Distance	Hits	Net	Miss	Short	U/K	Check	Time	Note
1								
2								
3								
4								
5								
6								
7								

Session 3: Rampart: _____ Attack/Defence: _____ .

Distance	Hits	Net	Miss	Short	U/K	Check	Time	Note
1								
2								
3								
4								
5								
6								
7								

Session 4: Rampart: _____ Attack/Defence: _____ .

Distance	Hits	Net	Miss	Short	U/K	Check	Time	Note
1								
2								
3								
4								
5								
6								
7								

Advanced Notice – At Site Entrances

Sling Defence Experiment

A sectiin the north-west of the Hillfort is being used today for an archaeology experiment. We are investigating how the development of the ramparts during the Iron Age would have affected its defence against attackers using sling stones.

Around 400 BC, many hillforts were rebuilt with multiple large ramparts and deep ditches replacing the smaller single rampart and ditch of the Early Iron Age. One theory is that the change was a response to attackers using slings; the new layout gave the defenders a greater height advantage and more time to use their own slings.

To test these ideas, we are slinging at targets in several positions on the ramparts, both "attacking" and "defending". We hope that the experience of using the defences and the scores of hits and misses will shed light on how the defences were used more than 2000 years ago.

The experiment involves slinging actual stones, so could be dangerous if you get too close. You may be asked to wait for a minute or two before walking through that area of the site.

Please look out for the warning sign near where the slinging is taking place, and observe the instructions on it. Slinging will be signalled by whistle – one blast means slinging is in progress, a double blast means "all clear".

Thank you for your co-operation.

Pete Robertson
University of Winchester
07767 XXXXXXX

Warning Notice

Warning

Sling Defence Experiment

Please wait here

This section of the Hillfort is being used for an experiment using sling stones, which could be dangerous if you get too close.

Please wait here until someone comes to show you a safe route to take. If no-one comes within a minute or so, please shout for attention; the slinging will stop until you have passed safely through.

A single whistle blast means that slinging is in progress; a double blast means "all clear" – the slinging has paused.

We apologise for any inconvenience; the delay should be only one or two minutes.

Thank you for your co-operation.

Participant Details Record (1)

Hillfort Defence Experiment Participant Details - Confidential

Participant Number:

Participant Name:

Contact Details:

Next of Kin/Emergency Contact:

Remarks:

This sheet to be kept separate and in confidence.

Participant Details Record (2)

Hillfort Defence Experiment Participant Details

Participant Number:

Date:

Previous Slinging Experience:

Stature:

Length Arm:

Weight:

Handedness:

Vision:

Sling Type (1):

Length:

Sling Type (2)

Length:

Footwear etc.:

Other Remarks:

Emergency Instructions

In the Event of an Emergency

The following information may be useful in the event of an emergency at Hod Hill.

Some mobile phone systems work at the site – e.g. O2 (Pete's phone); others may take 999 calls.
The site is: north-west corner of Hod Hill, near Stourpaine. Nearest town is Blandford Forum.
The grid reference for the site is: ST 854 109.

Blandford Community Hospital, Milldown Rd, has a "minor injuries" service. 01258 456541.
The nearest A&E departments: Poole General Hospital, Longfleet Rd, Poole. 01202 665511.
                                Dorset County Hospital, Williams Avenue, Dorchester. 01305 51150.

There are doctors' surgeries at: Barnes Close, Sturminster Newton, phone: 01258 474500.
                                    Upper Street, Child Okeford, phone: 01258 860687.
                                    White Cliff Mill Street, Blandford Forum, phone: 01258 452501.

The National Trust (landowner) contacts: Rob Rhodes (Property Manager) 01297 XXXXXX.
                                          Martin Papworth (Archaeologist) 01985 XXXXXX.

There are emergency contact details for slingers on the Participant Data sheets.
Pete's emergency contact is Elizabeth Robertson, 01794 XXXXXX.
Pete's car is a red Audi A4 estate, XXXX BMZ.

Location Map of Hod Hill Area

Safety Analysis and Plan

Iron Age Hillfort Defence Experiment Safety Plan

Introduction

This document describes the Safety analyses and procedures associated with an experiment to be conducted as part of an MRes Archaeology degree. It is intended to support the University of Winchester Safety Form B for the study. The USHA/UCEA document *Guidance on Health and Safety in Fieldwork*, May 2011, has been used as a guide in the preparation of this plan.

Overview of the experiment

The details of the experiment are described in the Methodology Paper that forms the main part of the plan for the study. However, a brief summary is included here for the convenience of reviewers.

The experiment involves experienced slingers (volunteers recruited from re-enactment groups) casting stones at a target placed at various positions on the defensive ramparts of an Iron Age hillfort.

Each slinger will use a simple sling to make 144 casts in sets of six, plus a few practice casts, over a period of a few hours on a single day. Half the casts will be from the top of the rampart, and the other half will be toward a target on the rampart from various positions in the defences. It will therefore be necessary for the participants to move across the rampart and ditch of the hillfort.

The hillfort to be used is Hod Hill, which is on National Trust property. A number of the details of the following result from requirements of the NT in reaching a formal agreement with them for the use of the site.

The site is 350m walk from the nearest road, and has public access. For the period of the trials notices will be used to warn visitors of the experiment and ask them to wait for a signal before passing through. The procedure requires a cessation of slinging while walkers or others are present.

Risk Analysis

The following safety risks have been identified (ref USHA/UCEA page 22):

1. Stone hitting participant, experimenter or observer, or passer-by

2. Stone hitting animal
3. Trips, slips, or falls on the ramparts
4. Muscle or joint injury due to slinging
5. Injury caused by carrying equipment
6. Illness or other problem not related to the experiment, but at what may be a remote site
7. Travel-related risks.

The likelihood and probable severity of each of these has been informally assessed and none of them judged to be out of the ordinary *for people who are already experienced slingers*.

For each, a twofold approach is proposed. First, the briefing and instructions draw participants' attention to the risks and advises how to take care to avoid them; they are also instructed to desist immediately should an incident occur or seem likely. (The travel risk is covered in the joining instructions provided to the participants.) Second, the written procedures for the experiment include steps to be taken to reduce the likelihood of occurrence, as described below.

Safety Procedures

1. Wherever relevant, the Archaeology department's standard practice for reviewing, conducting and recording safety-related matters will be used, including incident reports. (All risks.)
2. Everyone present at the experiment will receive a briefing that will include the safety procedures. (Risks 1-4 and 6.)
3. Participants will be instructed not to proceed if they have any safety-related concern, and will clearly be told that they may stop at any time. (All risks.)
4. The experimenter will check that participants are experienced and accurate slingers, and cease operation if not. Likewise if a participant shows unwillingness to follow the procedures. (Risks 1, 2 and 4.)
5. Whistles will be used to warn of the commencement of each series of casts, and to signal a cessation should passers-by or animals move into the area of operation. (Risks 1 and 2.)
6. Observers and anyone else present will be kept at a safe position and distance. (Risk 1.)
7. Members of the public will be excluded from the area. If passers-by cannot reliably be excluded, then warning signs will be used and an assistant will keep watch, signalling safe/unsafe conditions with a whistle. (Risk 1.)
8. The slinging area will exclude animals. Where this is not entirely possible (e.g. dogs being exercised), the keeping watch and whistle approach will be used. (Risk 2.)
9. Where it is necessary for participants to cross ramparts, they will be given plenty of time and be shown a safe route to take. Wet slopes will be avoided,

and suitable footwear encouraged. A stick (trekking pole) makes negotiating slopes easier and will be provided. (Risk 3.)
10. The experiment will be postponed in the event of bad weather. (Risk 3.)
11. A pilot experiment will be used to assess the terrain and any related issues. (Risk 3.)
12. A first aid kit will be available on site. (Risk 6.)
13. The route to the nearest hospital A&E department will be identified, and to a nearby doctor's surgery. Mobile phone coverage checked. (Risk 6.)
14. The arrangements for travel to the site will be reviewed for each participant, and if practical eased. (E.g. by providing a lift from a nearby station.) Joining instructions make it clear that participants should not hurry, even if late. (Risk 7.)
15. Depending on the experiment site chosen and a participant's address, consideration will be given to whether travel both to and from the site on the same day as the experiment is advisable. Any accommodation arrangements will be reviewed with the Supervisor, with reference to the Ethics policy. (Risk 7.)
16. The target is not yet constructed, but will be built with carrying in mind (light and foldable). Storage on-site will be requested, to reduce carrying. Other equipment is small or easily-divisible (bags of sling-stones). (Risk 5.)

Review

This Safety Plan has been independently reviewed. A Pilot Experiment (one slinger on one day, following the above procedures) tested the procedures and resulted in improvements to the instructions.

Exhibits

[The following pages showed the instructions and warning signs relevant to this plan; they are shown elsewhere in the Appendix.]

Ethics Analysis and Plan

Ethical Aspects of Iron Age Hillfort Defence Experiment

Introduction

This document describes ethics aspects of an experiment to be conducted as part of an archaeological investigation. It is intended to support the University of Winchester RKE Ethics Form for the study.

Overview of the experiment

The details of the experiment are described in the Methodology Paper that forms the main part of the plan for the study. However, a summary is included here for the convenience of reviewers.

The objective is to compare two types of Iron Age hillfort ramparts, that represent defences before and after a change of design in the fourth century BC. It is hypothesised that this change relates to sling warfare, improving defence against slings. In a broader context, these details may illuminate a current debate about the function of hillforts and their defences.

The experiment involves experienced slingers casting stones at targets in positions representative of attackers and defenders of Iron Age hillforts. It will compare their performance (hits on targets) at various distances and in attack versus defence, over two type of rampart. It will therefore be conducted at an actual hillfort (probably Hod Hill, Dorset).

The slingers will be volunteers recruited from re-enactment societies and through a slinging enthusiasts' website. It is necessary for the experiment that the slingers are experienced, and this also ensures that they can make an informed decision to participate. Their expertise is also an important aspect of ensuring their safety and that of observers during the experiment.

The experimenter will collect a small amount of pertinent personal information from the slingers in addition to the results of their casts – principally anthropometric data such as arm-length, and details of their previous slinging experience. Participants will also be invited to comment on the experiment and on the features of the hillfort. The data will be collected and reported in such a way that it is anonymous to all but the individual participant. One or two participants, however, will be asked for permission to photograph them in action, to illustrate the report; their wishes in this regard will of course be respected.

The objectives are to ensure that the experiment is conducted to a high ethical standard, that all relevant formal requirements are adhered to and that all participants and sites are treated with respect. The relevant sections of the IFA Code of Conduct (Institute for Archaeologists 2010) and the Code of Ethics of the Human Factors and Ergonomics Society (Human Factors and Ergonomics Society 2005) have been used as guides.

Ethics was considered as an integral factor during the design and planning for the experiment. The aspects identified in that process are described below.

The statistical design of the experiment calls for multiples of four participants; the expectation is that finding more than eight experienced volunteers is unlikely. The pilot run of the experiment will enable this to be checked for statistical adequacy, but a total of four or eight is expected to suffice.

Ethical Factors Influencing the Experimental Procedures

The following areas requiring consideration have been factored into the approach of the experiment:

Health and Safety risks to participants and others

A separate Safety Plan has been drafted and reviewed. Requirements imposed by the landowner will also be observed.

From the ethics perspective, the safety procedures will ensure that the participants are at no unusual risk; less than they would be at while pursuing slinging as a hobby or similar to exploring the ramparts of a hillfort during a country walk. Key points of these procedures are:

- A briefing that points out the identified risks and advises on how to avoid them
- Supervision by the experimenter
- The use of experienced slingers as participants
- Clear instructions that safety has priority and that slinging should stop immediately in any case of doubt.

Repetitive Testing can give rise to ethics issues, but in this case repletion is planned to simply be a matter of how much slinging is involved. To be explicit: I expect that each participant will sling 144 stones, in four sessions during the course of a single day. There will be breaks between the sessions, and the stones will be cast in sets of 6 with short breaks between them for the target to be moved. This degree of "repetition" is not out of the ordinary for a slinging enthusiast.

Embarrassments to participants

Some of the participants may be sensitive to it being known that they made errors or were less accurate in slinging than others. Their data will be treated in confidence in so far as individuals' results will be reported only to the individuals concerned, and the experiment will be conducted in a professional manner. (If participants elect to attend at the same time as acquaintances, they will in effect have chosen to allow their performance to be observed, but competitiveness will be discouraged.)

Deception of participants

There is no need to deceive the participants about the nature of the experiment. However, to avoid them thinking that the experimenter favours one result over another (and perhaps biasing their performance, consciously or otherwise), the instructions will simply refer to the experiment "comparing different rampart types" in general terms.

Motivation of participants

Participants will be asked to be as accurate as possible with every cast. Their motivation is their personal interest in slinging and in pre-historic use of slings. No payment to participants will be made. As some participants will travel several hundred miles to participate, the cost of simple B&B accommodation will be met. (This was reviewed with my Supervisor before being agreed.)

Handling participants' details

Individuals will be assigned participant numbers at random. There will be one record of this, separate from all the other record sheets, which will be held in confidence by the experimenter. Other data sheets will include only the participant number as identification. Therefore the performance data and the participants' details will not be identified with the individuals' names in the records and analyses. This arrangement also meets Data Protection requirements.

Feedback and acknowledgements to participants

Subsequent to the experiment, every participant will receive thanks, a summary of the overall results and a summary of their own data. Individuals who participate in informal trials will be acknowledged in the experiment report, as will groups (e.g. Slingers.org) which provide volunteers.

Exclusion of data

Selectively excluding data from the results could bias the outcome. Any decision to exclude data will be subject to independent review and will be mentioned in the report. (Examples might be if a participant was unable to complete all the trials, or declared that he was favouring one condition over another.)

Damage to environment

Every effort will be made to avoid damage to the site of the experiment, especially as an actual monument is involved. This will include observing all the requirements of the site-owner and permissions, instructions to participants regarding respect for the monument, avoiding erosion, and clearing up sling-stones and any other materials.

Independent Review

Independent review of the ethics of the experiment plan is planned and welcomed.

Documentation

[Exhibits of the instructions to participants were shown below.]

Equipment

The figures in this section show more details of the experiment equipment: a comparison of the size of the target net to a group of opponents (Figure 70); the consistency of the clay shot (Figure 71); the damage caused by stone sling-shot (Figures 72 and 73).

FIGURE 70. THE TARGET REPRESENTED A GROUP OF OPPONENTS.

FIGURE 71. CLAY SHOT BROKEN BY IMPACT ON TARGET.

FIGURE 72. HOLE IN NET CAUSED BY SLING-STONE.

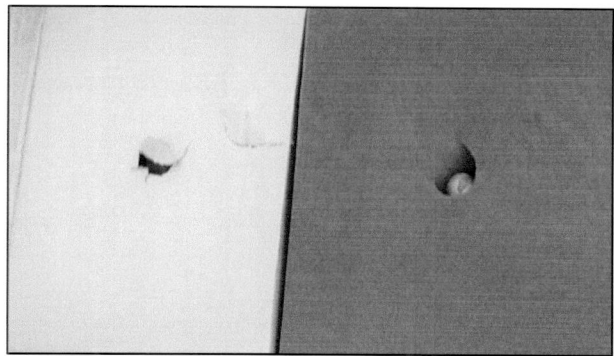

FIGURE 73. SLING-STONE HAVING PENETRATED
CARDBOARD AND FOAM.

Appendix B: Experiment Results and Data Analyses

Participant Data

The data collected from each participant are summarised in Figure 74.

The sling types were: 1 riveted leather pouch, modern braided cord; 2 'York replica' – leather pouch and jute string; 3 leather pouch and plaited leather cord; 4 Andean – braided alpaca wool cords and split pouch.

Raw Slinging Data

The raw data of the hits of various types and timing for sets of six casts at each position is shown in Figure 75 for the first six participants and in Figure 76 for Participants 1A-1D and 7. The tables also show presentation order of conditions and target distance for each position.

Participant	Slinging Experience (Yrs/Sessions)			Stature	Arm Length (cm)	Sling Length (cm)	Vision (General and Binocular)	Age	Handedness	Sling Type	Footwear Check
	Total Years	In Last Year	In Last Month								
1	28	>50	2	5' 6" 168cm	59.5	82	OK	44	R	1	OK
2	4	12	1	6' 1" 185cm	68.5	64.5	OK	40	R	2	OK
3	1.1	1	0	6' 2" 188cm	67.5	60	OK	40	R	3	OK
4	1	3	0	6' 2" 188cm	65.0	79	OK	24	R	3	OK
5	23	1	0	5'9" 175cm	60.0	77	Good	38	R*	3	OK
6	0.9	3	0	5' 10" 178cm	69.0	82	Good	27	L	3	OK
7	14	5	1	6' 6" 198cm	82.0	98.5	OK	50	R	4	OK

*Participant 5 was naturally left-handed but trained to use re-enactment weapons right-handed.

FIGURE 74. PARTICIPANT DATA.

P'pant:			All		1						2						3					
Rampart	Mode	Pos.	Total	Mean	Order	Nsl	Hit	Head	Total	Time	Order	Nsl	Hit	Head	Total	Time	Order	Nsl	Hit	Head	Total	Time
Uni	Attack	1	28	4.00	1	4	0	0	4	37.4	2	2	0	0	2	30.5	-					
Uni	Attack	2	36	5.14		4	2	1	6	46.2		3	1	0	4	27.2						
Uni	Attack	3	40	5.71		0	6	2	6	40.0		2	3	0	5	26.0						
Uni	Attack	4	39	5.57		1	5	2	6	34.2		5	1	0	6	27.4						
Uni	Attack	5	37	5.29		1	5	1	6	36.4		3	1	0	4	28.4						
Uni	Defend	1	28	4.00	2	3	2	0	5	34.0	1	3	1	0	4	31.0	-					
Uni	Defend	2	32	4.57		2	4	0	6	34.4		4	1	0	5	33.6						
Uni	Defend	3	35	5.00		4	1	0	5	34.0		5	1	0	6	29.5						
Uni	Defend	4	32	4.57		4	2	0	6	29.5		2	2	1	4	30.0						
Uni	Defend	5	37	5.29		3	3	0	6	28.1		4	2	0	6	27.6						
Bi	Attack	1	5	0.45	3	0	0	0	0	34.0	4	0	0	0	0	50.0	1	0	0	0	0	76.4
Bi	Attack	2	16	1.45		1	0	0	1	42.8		0	0	0	0	44.5		0	0	0	0	67.0
Bi	Attack	4	1	0.09		0	0	0	0	39.0		0	0	0	0	51.9		0	0	0	0	80.0
Bi	Attack	6	24	2.18		5	0	0	5	29.6		1	0	0	1	34.0		0	0	0	0	85.0
Bi	Attack	7	28	2.55		3	0	0	3	32.4		3	0	0	3	36.0		1	0	0	1	85.0
Bi	Attack	8	29	2.64		5	0	0	5	30.0		3	1	0	4	31.8		1	0	0	1	69.0
Bi	Attack	9	43	3.91		4	2	0	6	25.6		3	1	0	4	33.0		2	0	0	2	67.0
Bi	Defend	1	11	1.10	4	2	0	0	2	34.2	3	0	0	0	0	36.5	2	0	0	0	0	55.0
Bi	Defend	2	13	1.30		0	0	0	0	34.0		2	0	0	2	35.6		0	0	0	0	80.0
Bi	Defend	4	17	1.89		0	0	0	0	42.0		2	0	0	2	36.0						
Bi	Defend	6	23	2.30		3	1	1	4	33.0		1	0	0	1	36.6		0	0	0	0	73.0
Bi	Defend	7	25	2.78		4	0	0	4	31.9		0	1	0	1	32.6						
Bi	Defend	8	27	3.00		3	0	0	3	28.4		0	0	0	0	31.4						
Bi	Defend	9	36	4.00		1	1	0	2	31.6		1	1	0	2	35.4						
	Totals:		642			57	34	7	91	823		49	17	1	66	817		4	0	0	4	737
	Means:		3.01			2.38	1.42	0.29	3.79	34.3		2.04	0.71	0.04	2.75	34.0		0.40	0.00	0.00	0.40	73.7

P'pant:			4						5						6					
Rampart	Mode	Pos.	Order	Nsl	Hit	Head	Total	Time	Order	Nsl	Hit	Head	Total	Time	Order	Nsl	Hit	Head	Total	Time
Uni	Attack	1	-						-						-					
Uni	Attack	2																		
Uni	Attack	3																		
Uni	Attack	4																		
Uni	Attack	5																		
Uni	Defend	1	-						-						-					
Uni	Defend	2																		
Uni	Defend	3																		
Uni	Defend	4																		
Uni	Defend	5																		
Bi	Attack	1	1	0	0	0	0	64.0	2	0	0	0	0		2	0	0	0	0	
Bi	Attack	2		0	0	0	0	79.4		0	0	0	0			0	0	0	0	
Bi	Attack	4		0	0	0	0	85.0		0	0	0	0			1	0	0	1	
Bi	Attack	6		0	0	0	0	84.0		1	0	0	1			1	0	0	1	
Bi	Attack	7		2	0	0	2	96.0		0	0	0	0			0	0	0	0	
Bi	Attack	8		0	1	0	1	77.0		0	0	0	0			0	1	1	1	
Bi	Attack	9		2	2	1	4	80.0		2	1	1	3			1	0	0	1	
Bi	Defend	1	2	1	0	0	1	72.0	1	0	0	0	0	70.0	1	1	0	0	1	94.0
Bi	Defend	2		1	0	0	1	73.0		0	0	0	0	72.0		0	0	0	0	97.0
Bi	Defend	4		1	1	0	2	67.0		0	0	0	0	61.0		3	0	0	3	
Bi	Defend	6		4	0	0	4	79.0		1	0	0	1	62.0		1	0	0	1	100
Bi	Defend	7		1	0	0	1	65.0		0	0	0	0	55.0		3	0	0	3	81.0
Bi	Defend	8		2	1	0	3			1	0	0	1			1	0	0	1	
Bi	Defend	9		6	0	0	6			4	0	0	4			3	0	0	3	
	Totals:			20	5	1	25	921		9	1	1	10	320		15	1	1	16	372
	Means:			1.43	0.36	0.07	1.79	76.8		0.64	0.07	0.07	0.71	64.0		1.07	0.07	0.07	1.14	93.0

FIGURE 75. RAW DATA FOR PARTICIPANTS 1-6.

P'pant:			All		1A						1B						1C						1D						7			Range
Flagnumber	Mode	Pos.	Total	Mean	Order	No.	Hit	Head	Total	Time	Order	No.	Hit	Head	Total	Time	Order	No.	Hit	Head	Total	Time	Order	No.	Hit	Head	Total	Time	No.	Hit	Head	Total	Time	
Uni	Attack	1	28	4.00	1	4	1	0	5	33.0	1	4	2	0	6	33.0	4	4	2	0	6	33.0		3	4	0	5	33.0	2	0	0	0	62.0	19.8
Uni	Attack	2	36	5.14		2	4	0	6	32.5		2	4	0	6	32.5		2	3	1	5	32.0		3	3	0	6	32.0	2	1	0	3	70.0	13.8
Uni	Attack	3	40	5.71		4	2	0	6	29.0		4	2	0	6	29.0		1	5	0	6	30.5		3	3	1	6	30.5	2	3	0	5	64.0	11.3
Uni	Attack	4	39	5.57		2	4	1	6	26.0		3	3	0	6	26.0		1	5	0	6	31.5		1	5	2	6	31.5	1	2	0	3	90.0	9.4
Uni	Attack	5	37	5.29		1	5	1	6	30.5		3	3	0	6	30.5		5	1	0	6	33.0		2	3	0	5	33.0	2	2	0	4	95.0	7.2
Uni	Defend	1	28	4.00		4	1	0	5	29.0	3	3	2	0	5	29.0	3	3	1	0	4	31.5		1	2	1	3	31.5	2	2	0	2	78.0	20.0
Uni	Defend	2	32	4.57	2	1	5	4	6	29.0		2	3	1	6	29.0		3	3	0	6	32.0		2	4	1	6	32.0	0	0	0	0	65.0	13.8
Uni	Defend	3	35	5.00		3	3	0	6	29.0		2	2	2	6	29.0		4	2	1	5	31.5		2	4	0	5	31.5	2	2	0	2	71.0	11.1
Uni	Defend	4	32	4.57		3	1	0	4	27.0		3	3	2	6	27.0		4	2	2	6	32.5		4	1	1	5	32.5	2	2	0	2	59.0	9.4
Uni	Defend	5	37	5.29		1	5	1	6	28.5		4	2	0	6	28.5		3	6	4	6	31.0		3	3	1	6	31.0	1	1	0	1	56.0	7.5
Bi	Attack	1	5	0.45	3	0	0	0	0	33.0	3	1	0	0	1	33.0	2	0	0	0	0	33.0		3	1	0	4	33.0	0	0	0	0	74.0	46.2
Bi	Attack	2	16	1.45		4	1	0	5	35.0		2	1	0	3	35.0	2	2	1	0	3	33.0		3	0	0	3	33.0	1	0	0	1	79.0	40.4
Bi	Attack	4	1	0.09		0	0	0	0	37.0		0	0	0	0	37.0		0	0	0	0	34.0		3	0	1	0	34.0	0	0	0	0	81.0	37.3
Bi	Attack	6	24	2.18		3	0	0	3	38.0		3	2	0	5	38.0		0	0	0	2	32.0		0	1	0	4	32.0	2	1	0	2	77.0	25.9
Bi	Attack	7	28	2.55		4	1	0	5	29.5		4	0	0	5	29.5		2	1	0	3	31.5		3	2	0	5	31.5	1	0	0	1	77.0	22.6
Bi	Attack	8	29	2.64		2	0	0	2	30.0		5	0	0	5	30.0		3	1	0	4	31.5		4	0	0	4	31.5	2	2	0	2	76.0	19.3
Bi	Attack	9	43	3.91		2	4	0	6	30.5		4	2	0	6	30.5		2	4	0	6	33.0		3	0	0	4	33.0	0	1	1	1	76.0	11.8
Bi	Defend	1	11	1.10	4	2	1	0	3	32.0	4	0	1	0	1	32.0	1	1	0	0	1	36.0		1	1	0	2	36.0						46.4
Bi	Defend	2	13	1.30		1	0	0	1	33.0		4	1	0	5	33.0		1	0	0	1	32.5		3	0	0	3	32.5						40.4
Bi	Defend	4	17	1.89		0	0	0	0	33.5		1	0	0	1	33.5		3	0	0	4	31.5		4	0	0	4	31.5						37.3
Bi	Defend	6	23	2.30		3	2	0	5	30.0		4	0	0	4	30.0		1	0	0	1	32.0		1	1	0	2	32.0						25.9
Bi	Defend	7	25	2.78		3	1	0	4	32.0		3	2	0	5	32.0		4	1	0	5	32.5		1	1	0	2	32.5						22.0
Bi	Defend	8	27	3.00		2	2	0	4	33.0		3	1	0	4	33.0		4	1	1	5	32.5		5	1	1	6	32.5						19.3
Bi	Defend	9	36	4.00		4	1	0	5	29.5		2	4	3	6	29.5		2	2	1	4	31.0		1	3	1	4	31.0						12.1
Totals:			642			55	44	7	99	750		63	44	10	107	750		51	43	17	94	775		57	44	10	101	775	20	9	0	29	1250	
Means:			3.01			2.29	1.83	0.29	4.13	31.2		2.63	1.83	0.42	4.46	31.2		2.13	1.79	0.71	3.92	32.3		2.38	1.83	0.42	4.21	32.3	1.18	0.53	0.00	1.71	73.5	

FIGURE 76. RAW DATA FOR PARTICIPANTS 1A–1D AND 7.

APPENDIX B: EXPERIMENT RESULTS AND DATA ANALYSES   111

Analyses of Variance

The accuracy data were subjected to multivariate analyses of variance using the IBM Statistical Package for the Social Sciences 19 (SPSS). To take advantage of the repeated measures design, the analysis chosen was the General Linear Model Repeated Measures option as described by Gray and Kinnear (2012: 336-346). The analysis compared Hits and Total Hits for 'position' across the 'rampart-type' and 'attack/defend' main conditions. The SPSS summary tables are shown below, in Figures 77 and 78.

This analysis requires that the data are collected from subjects who experienced all the conditions being compared, and therefore only data from Participants 1, 1A-1D and 2 were used. A further requirement of the analysis is for equal numbers of levels within the main factors. That is, it is not possible to compare the Univallate/Bivallate results across all the positions trialled as there were five positions in the univallate case and seven in the bivallate case. Two sets of positions were considered to be comparable, and a separate analysis was conducted for each. See Figure 35 for illustrations of the positions.

The first set analysed was Positions 1, 2 and 4 for both ramparts, because their location 'on the ground' was the same in the two cases. That is, this analysis compares performance for slinging from and against the positions just outside the hillfort, on the counterscarp bank and in the outer ditch.

The second set analysed was Positions 2, 3, 4 and 5 of the univallate case against Positions 6, 7, 8 and 9 of the bivallate case. That is, this analysis compares performance for slinging from and against the four positions at the lip, bottom and two slopes of the ditch below the rampart in question, that is, similar positions relative to the defenders.

The results of the 'Same on the Ground' analysis show the effect of rampart type (univallate versus bivallate) to be statistically significant for both Hits and Total Hits. For Hits: $F(1, 5) = 71.49$; $p < .001$. For Total Hits: $F(1, 5) = 110.00$; $p < .001$.

The effect of Position was not significant on the Hits measure but was significant on the Total Hits measure. For Total Hits: $F(2, 10) = 6.69$; $p = .014$.

The Attack/Defend effect was not significant on either measure. However, the interaction between Attack/Defend and Rampart type was significant on the Total Hits measure. For Total Hits: $F(1, 5) = 10.25$; $p = .024$.

The Rampart x Position interaction was significant on the Hits measure. For Hits: $F(2, 10) = 4.52$; $p = .040$.

None of the other 'same on the ground' interactions was significant on either measure at the $p < .05$ criterion.

The results of the 'Same Position Relative to Defenders' analysis also showed a significant effect of rampart type on both measures. For Hits: $F(1, 5) = 37.50$; $p = .002$. For Total Hits: $F(1, 5) = 32.22$; $p = .02$.

The effect of Position was significant on the Hits measure. For Hits: $F(3, 15) = 12.11$; $p < .001$.

The Attack/Defend effect was significant on the Total Hits measure only. For Total Hits: $F(1, 5) = 11.35$; $p = .02$.

None of the interactions was significant in the case of position relative to defenders.

The tables below are the output from the multivariate analyses of variance from SPSS.

Source	Measure	Type III Sum of Squares	df	Mean Square	F	Sig.	Partial Eta Squared
Rampart	Hits	80.222	1	80.222	71.485	.000	.935
	Total_Hits	242.000	1	242.000	110.000	.000	.957
Error(Rampart)	Hits	5.611	5	1.122			
	Total_Hits	11.000	5	2.200			
Attack_Defend	Hits	.500	1	.500	.833	.403	.143
	Total_Hits	.222	1	.222	.357	.576	.067
Error(Attack_Defend)	Hits	3.000	5	.600			
	Total_Hits	3.111	5	.622			
Position	Hits	5.333	2	2.667	3.137	.088	.386
	Total_Hits	12.111	2	6.056	6.687	.014	.572
Error(Position)	Hits	8.500	10	.850			
	Total_Hits	9.056	10	.906			
Rampart * Attack_Defend	Hits	1.389	1	1.389	1.276	.310	.203
	Total_Hits	6.722	1	6.722	10.254	.024	.672
Error(Rampart*Attack_Defend)	Hits	5.444	5	1.089			
	Total_Hits	3.278	5	.656			
Rampart * Position	Hits	5.778	2	2.889	4.522	.040	.475
	Total_Hits	6.333	2	3.167	1.845	.208	.270
Error(Rampart*Position)	Hits	6.389	10	.639			
	Total_Hits	17.167	10	1.717			
Attack_Defend * Position	Hits	1.000	2	.500	.476	.635	.087
	Total_Hits	2.111	2	1.056	.554	.591	.100
Error(Attack_Defend*Position)	Hits	10.500	10	1.050			
	Total_Hits	19.056	10	1.906			
Rampart * Attack_Defend * Position	Hits	4.111	2	2.056	2.270	.154	.312
	Total_Hits	8.444	2	4.222	2.005	.185	.286
Error(Rampart*Attack_Defend*Position)	Hits	9.056	10	.906			
	Total_Hits	21.056	10	2.106			

FIGURE 77. ANOVA FOR 'SAME ON THE GROUND' POSITIONS.

Source	Measure	Type III Sum of Squares	df	Mean Square	F	Sig.	Partial Eta Squared
Rampart	Hits	84.375	1	84.375	37.500	.002	.882
	Total_Hits	75.260	1	75.260	32.226	.002	.866
Error(Rampart)	Hits	11.250	5	2.250			
	Total_Hits	11.677	5	2.335			
Attack_Defend	Hits	3.375	1	3.375	5.625	.064	.529
	Total_Hits	5.510	1	5.510	11.352	.020	.694
Error(Attack_Defend)	Hits	3.000	5	.600			
	Total_Hits	2.427	5	.485			
Position	Hits	33.000	3	11.000	12.110	.000	.708
	Total_Hits	10.115	3	3.372	3.171	.055	.388
Error(Position)	Hits	13.625	15	.908			
	Total_Hits	15.948	15	1.063			
Rampart * Attack_Defend	Hits	4.167	1	4.167	4.202	.096	.457
	Total_Hits	1.260	1	1.260	.795	.413	.137
Error(Rampart*Attack_Defend)	Hits	4.958	5	.992			
	Total_Hits	7.927	5	1.585			
Rampart * Position	Hits	3.125	3	1.042	1.524	.249	.234
	Total_Hits	4.281	3	1.427	2.134	.139	.299
Error(Rampart*Position)	Hits	10.250	15	.683			
	Total_Hits	10.031	15	.669			
Attack_Defend * Position	Hits	3.458	3	1.153	.780	.523	.135
	Total_Hits	.365	3	.122	.096	.961	.019
Error(Attack_Defend*Position)	Hits	22.167	15	1.478			
	Total_Hits	18.948	15	1.263			
Rampart * Attack_Defend * Position	Hits	6.000	3	2.000	1.159	.358	.188
	Total_Hits	5.615	3	1.872	1.817	.187	.267
Error(Rampart*Attack_Defend*Position)	Hits	25.875	15	1.725			
	Total_Hits	15.448	15	1.030			

FIGURE 78. ANOVA FOR 'RELATIVE TO DEFENDERS' POSITIONS.

Descriptive Statistics

The following tables, Figures 79 and 80, are also output from the SPSS analysis. They provide means, standard deviations and confidence limits for the hit rates of the main conditions within the two comparisons ('Same on the Ground' and 'Relative to Defenders') for Participants 1-1D and 2. The numbers represent hits per set of six shots, in each case. (Note that position numbers in these analyses refer to the conditions statistically compared: the 'Descriptive Statistics' sub-tables indicate what those slinging positions were, as defined in Chapter 5.)

Same on The Ground

Descriptive Statistics

	Mean	Std. Deviation	N
UA1	1.83	1.835	6
UA2	2.83	1.169	6
UA4	3.17	1.835	6
UD1	1.50	.548	6
UD2	3.17	1.472	6
UD4	1.83	.753	6
BA1	.17	.408	6
BA2	.50	.548	6
BA4	.00	.000	6
BD1	.50	.548	6
BD2	.17	.408	6
BD4	.33	.516	6
UA1	4.67	1.506	6
UA2	5.50	.837	6
UA4	6.00	.000	6
UD1	4.33	.816	6
UD2	5.33	1.211	6
UD4	5.00	.894	6
BA1	.83	1.602	6
BA2	2.50	1.761	6
BA4	.00	.000	6
BD1	1.50	1.049	6
BD2	2.00	1.789	6
BD4	2.00	2.098	6

Grand Mean

Measure	Mean	Std. Error	95% Confidence Interval	
			Lower Bound	Upper Bound
Hits	1.333	.191	.842	1.825
Total_Hits	3.306	.221	2.737	3.874

Rampart Estimates

Measure	Rampart	Mean	Std. Error	95% Confidence Interval	
				Lower Bound	Upper Bound
Hits	1	2.389	.309	1.594	3.184
	2	.278	.093	.039	.517
Total_Hits	1	5.139	.199	4.627	5.651
	2	1.472	.345	.584	2.360

Attack/Defend Estimates

Measure	Attack_Defend	Mean	Std. Error	95% Confidence Interval	
				Lower Bound	Upper Bound
Hits	1	1.417	.275	.711	2.123
	2	1.250	.120	.942	1.558
Total_Hits	1	3.250	.297	2.486	4.014
	2	3.361	.163	2.941	3.781

Position Estimates

Measure	Position	Mean	Std. Error	95% Confidence Interval	
				Lower Bound	Upper Bound
Hits	1	1.000	.289	.258	1.742
	2	1.667	.271	.969	2.364
	3	1.333	.154	.938	1.728
Total_Hits	1	2.833	.293	2.079	3.588
	2	3.833	.293	3.079	4.588
	3	3.250	.224	2.675	3.825

FIGURE 79. DETAILS FOR SAME ON THE GROUND ANALYSIS (5-PART FIGURE).

Relative to Defenders

Descriptive Statistics

	Mean	Std. Deviation	N
UA2	2.83	1.169	6
UA3	3.50	1.643	6
UA4	3.17	1.835	6
UA5	4.00	1.673	6
UD2	3.17	1.472	6
UD3	1.83	.983	6
UD4	1.83	.753	6
UD5	3.50	1.643	6
BA6	.50	.837	6
BA7	.83	.753	6
BA8	.33	.516	6
BA9	2.67	1.211	6
BD6	.67	.816	6
BD7	1.00	.632	6
BD8	.83	.753	6
BD9	2.00	1.265	6
UA2	5.50	.837	6
UA3	5.83	.408	6
UA4	6.00	.000	6
UA5	5.50	.837	6
UD2	5.33	1.211	6
UD3	5.50	.548	6
UD4	5.00	.894	6
UD5	6.00	.000	6
BA6	3.33	1.633	6
BA7	4.00	1.095	6
BA8	4.00	1.095	6
BA9	5.33	1.033	6
BD6	2.83	1.722	6
BD7	3.50	1.643	6
BD8	3.67	2.066	6
BD9	3.83	1.602	6

Grand Mean

Measure	Mean	Std. Error	95% Confidence Interval	
			Lower Bound	Upper Bound
Hits	2.042	.220	1.476	2.607
Total_Hits	4.698	.256	4.040	5.356

Rampart Estimates

Measure	Rampart	Mean	Std. Error	95% Confidence Interval	
				Lower Bound	Upper Bound
Hits	1	2.979	.325	2.144	3.815
	2	1.104	.195	.604	1.605
Total_Hits	1	5.583	.124	5.266	5.901
	2	3.812	.405	2.770	4.855

Attack/Defend Estimates

Measure	Attack_Defend	Mean	Std. Error	95% Confidence Interval	
				Lower Bound	Upper Bound
Hits	1	2.229	.247	1.595	2.863
	2	1.854	.220	1.289	2.419
Total_Hits	1	4.938	.247	4.302	5.573
	2	4.458	.283	3.732	5.185

Position Estimates

Measure	Position	Mean	Std. Error	95% Confidence Interval	
				Lower Bound	Upper Bound
Hits	1	1.792	.312	.989	2.595
	2	1.792	.136	1.443	2.140
	3	1.542	.119	1.235	1.848
	4	3.042	.420	1.961	4.122
Total_Hits	1	4.250	.387	3.254	5.246
	2	4.708	.253	4.057	5.360
	3	4.667	.300	3.894	5.439
	4	5.167	.300	4.394	5.939

FIGURE 80. DETAILS FOR RELATIVE TO DEFENDERS ANALYSIS (5-PART FIGURE).

Details of Results

Time of Assault

Figure 81 shows the length of time that an attacker would be exposed to defensive slinging, in each section of the defences, according to the speed assumptions adopted in the Tactical Analysis.

Position	Speed		
	Basic	Fast	Slow
UA1	12.0	8.0	13.0
UA2	0.5	0.3	1.0
UA3	1.0	0.8	1.5
UA4	0.5	0.4	1.0
UA5	4.0	3.0	5.0
UD1	12.0	8.0	13.0
UD2	0.5	0.3	1.0
UD3	1.0	0.8	1.5
UD4	0.5	0.4	1.0
UD5	4.0	3.0	5.0
BA1	12.0	8.0	13.0
BA2	0.5	0.3	1.0
BA4	6.5	5.2	8.5
BA6	1.0	0.5	1.5
BA7	3.5	2.5	5.0
BA8	1.0	0.8	1.5
BA9	13.0	10.0	15.0
BD1	12.0	8.0	13.0
BD2	0.5	0.3	1.0
BD4	6.5	5.2	8.5
BD6	1.0	0.5	1.5
BD7	3.5	2.5	5.0
BD8	1.0	0.8	1.5
BD9	13.0	10.0	15.0
Time for Whole Run:			
Univallate	18.0	12.5	21.5
Bivallate	37.5	27.3	45.5

FIGURE 81. EXPOSURE TIMES OF ATTACKERS BY AREA OF THE DEFENCES (SECONDS).

Accuracy and Slinging Time

The following tables expand Figure 48 (Average Hit Rates by Condition) by position, for all participants (Figure 82) and for Participant 1-1D (Figure 83). Figure 84 gives details of the timing of the slinging.

Effective Range

The result of each cast in the effective range trial is shown in Figure 85; Figure 86 shows the *effective* range against the hillfort profile, compared to the Finney's results for *maximum* range, at the same site (Finney 2006: 143); axis distances are relative to the survey datum for Figure 35.

Tactical Analyses

Figure 87 shows the *probability* that a given attacker would suffer or achieve a hit. The table also shows where the attacker would have reached, at the point of 50% probability of a hit. ('Face' means the outer slope of the rampart being defended.)

Figure 88 shows the probability of 'succeeding,' not of being hit. For example, if each hit has a 50% probability of incapacitating him, a Basic-speed attacker using Tactic 2 has an 18% chance of reaching the univallate rampart or a 30% chance of reaching the bivallate inner rampart.

Rampart	Attack/Defence	Position	Range	Shots	Heads	Hits	Nets	Total	%Heads	%Hits	%Nets	%Total
Univallate	A	1	19.8	42	2	11	17	28	4.8	26.2	40.5	66.7
	A	2	13.8	42	3	18	18	36	7.1	42.9	42.9	85.7
	A	3	11.3	42	3	24	16	40	7.1	57.1	38.1	95.2
	A	4	9.4	42	7	21	18	39	16.7	50.0	42.9	92.9
	A	5	7.2	42	7	26	11	37	16.7	61.9	26.2	88.1
	D	1	20.0	42	1	9	19	28	2.4	21.4	45.2	66.7
	D	2	13.8	42	7	19	13	32	16.7	45.2	31.0	76.2
	D	3	11.1	42	4	11	24	35	9.5	26.2	57.1	83.3
	D	4	9.4	42	5	11	21	32	11.9	26.2	50.0	76.2
	D	5	7.5	42	6	21	16	37	14.3	50.0	38.1	88.1
Bivallate	A	1	46.2	66	0	1	4	5	0.0	1.5	6.1	7.6
	A	2	40.4	66	0	3	13	16	0.0	4.5	19.7	24.2
	A	4	37.3	66	0	0	1	1	0.0	0.0	1.5	1.5
	A	6	25.9	66	0	3	21	24	0.0	4.5	31.8	36.4
	A	7	22.6	66	0	5	23	28	0.0	7.6	34.8	42.4
	A	8	19.3	66	1	4	25	29	1.5	6.1	37.9	43.9
	A	9	11.8	66	4	20	23	43	6.1	30.3	34.8	65.2
	D	1	46.4	60	0	3	8	11	0.0	5.0	13.3	18.3
	D	2	40.4	60	0	1	12	13	0.0	1.7	20.0	21.7
	D	4	37.3	54	0	3	14	17	0.0	5.6	25.9	31.5
	D	6	25.9	60	1	4	19	23	1.7	6.7	31.7	38.3
	D	7	22.0	54	1	6	19	25	1.9	11.1	35.2	46.3
	D	8	19.3	54	2	6	21	27	3.7	11.1	38.9	50.0
	D	9	12.1	54	5	12	24	36	9.3	22.2	44.4	66.7
Totals					59	242	400	642	4.6	18.9	31.3	50.2	1278

FIGURE 82. HITS BY POSITION, ALL PARTICIPANTS.

Figure 89 shows the effect of reinforcements, as discussed in the Scenario 2 tactical analysis above.

Rampart	Attack/Defence	Position	Range	Shots	Heads	Hits	Nets	Total	%Heads	%Hits	%Nets	%Total
Uni	A	1	19.8	30	2	11	15	26	6.7	36.7	50.0	86.7
Uni	A	2	13.8	30	3	16	13	29	10.0	53.3	43.3	96.7
Uni	A	3	11.3	30	3	18	12	30	10.0	60.0	40.0	100.0
Uni	A	4	9.4	30	7	18	12	30	23.3	60.0	40.0	100.0
Uni	A	5	7.2	30	7	23	6	29	23.3	76.7	20.0	96.7
Uni	D	1	20.0	30	1	8	14	22	3.3	26.7	46.7	73.3
Uni	D	2	13.8	30	7	18	9	27	23.3	60.0	30.0	90.0
Uni	D	3	11.1	30	4	10	17	27	13.3	33.3	56.7	90.0
Uni	D	4	9.4	30	4	9	17	26	13.3	30.0	56.7	86.7
Uni	D	5	7.5	30	6	19	11	30	20.0	63.3	36.7	100.0
Bi	A	1	46.2	30	0	1	4	5	0.0	3.3	13.3	16.7
Bi	A	2	40.4	30	0	3	12	15	0.0	10.0	40.0	50.0
Bi	A	4	37.3	30	0	0	0	0	0.0	0.0	0.0	0.0
Bi	A	6	25.9	30	0	3	16	19	0.0	10.0	53.3	63.3
Bi	A	7	22.6	30	0	5	16	21	0.0	16.7	53.3	70.0
Bi	A	8	19.3	30	0	1	19	20	0.0	3.3	63.3	66.7
Bi	A	9	11.8	30	2	15	13	28	6.7	50.0	43.3	93.3
Bi	D	1	46.4	30	0	3	6	9	0.0	10.0	20.0	30.0
Bi	D	2	40.4	30	0	1	9	10	0.0	3.3	30.0	33.3
Bi	D	4	37.3	30	0	2	8	10	0.0	6.7	26.7	33.3
Bi	D	6	25.9	30	1	4	12	16	3.3	13.3	40.0	53.3
Bi	D	7	22.0	30	1	5	15	20	3.3	16.7	50.0	66.7
Bi	D	8	19.3	30	2	5	17	22	6.7	16.7	56.7	73.3
Bi	D	9	12.1	30	5	11	10	21	16.7	36.7	33.3	70.0
Totals				720	55	209	283	492	7.6	29.0	39.3	68.3

FIGURE 83. HITS BY POSITION, PARTICIPANT 1-1D.

Position	All P's	P1-1D & 2	P1-1D	Position	All P's	P1-1D & 2	P1-1D
UA1	37.4	33.3	33.9	UD1	37.7	31.0	31.0
UA2	38.9	33.7	35.0	UD2	36.4	31.7	31.3
UA3	35.6	30.8	31.8	UD3	36.5	30.8	31.0
UA4	38.1	29.4	29.8	UD4	33.9	29.8	29.7
UA5	41.0	32.0	32.7	UD5	33.0	29.1	29.4
BA1	47.8	36.0	33.2	BD1	49.8	34.5	34.0
BA2	49.9	37.2	35.8	BD2	52.3	33.4	33.0
BA4	53.2	38.8	36.2	BD4	42.0	34.7	34.4
BA6	50.0	33.9	33.9	BD6	50.8	32.3	31.4
BA7	49.8	31.7	30.9	BD7	43.8	32.3	32.2
BA8	45.2	30.8	30.6	BD8	31.8	31.8	31.9
BA9	45.4	30.9	30.5	BD9	31.3	31.3	30.5

FIGURE 84. AVERAGE TIME FOR SIX CASTS BY POSITION (SECONDS).

Appendix B: Experiment Results and Data Analyses

Distance		Golf Ball	Dried Clay	Stone	Comment
40m	Staff Sl.	Over	Over	Over	Only just over
	Sling	Well over	Close	Close	
	Sling	Well over	Over	Over	
50m	Staff Sl.	Short	Just short	Hit	
	Sling	Well over	Close	Over	
	Sling	Well over	Over	Over	
60m	Staff Sl.	Short	Just short	Short	1st 2 hit on bounce
	Sling	Well over	Close	Short	
	Sling	Over	Hit	Close	
70m	Staff Sl.	Short	Short	Short	Low aim, not range
	Sling	Over	Very Close	Short	3rd hit on bounce
	Sling	Over	Over	Miss	

Figure 85. Results of Effective Range Informal Trial.

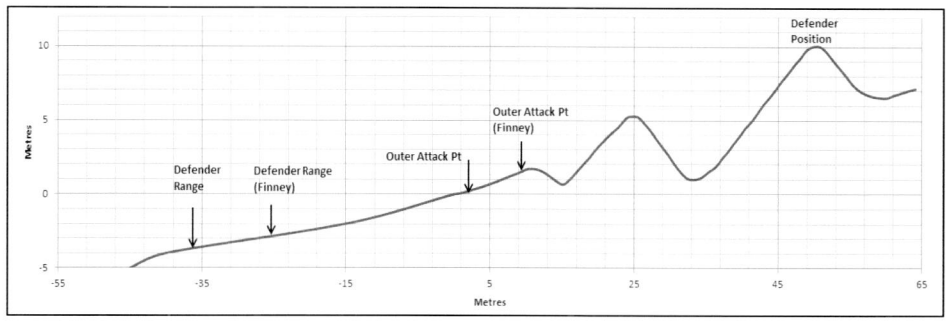

Figure 86. Effective Range Compared to Finney (2006).

Speed	Tactic	Probability Attacker Hit (%)	50% Position	Probability Defender Hit (%)	50% Position
			Univallate		
Basic	T1	99	Outside	99	Counterscarp
	T2	99	Counterscarp	96	Counterscarp
	T3	80	Low on face	0	None
Fast	T1	99	Counterscarp	99	Counterscarp
	T2	98	Counterscarp	96	Counterscarp
	T3	73	Middle of face	0	None
Slow	T1	>99	Outside	99	Counterscarp
	T2	99	Counterscarp	96	Counterscarp
	T3	86	Low on face	0	None
			Bivallate		
Basic	T1	96	Outer rampart	68	Middle of face
	T2	93	Inner ditch	61	High on ditto
	T3	83	Middle of face	0	None
Fast	T1	92	Inner Rampart	68	Middle of face
	T2	88	Inner ditch	61	High on face
	T3	72	Middle of face	0	None
Slow	T1	96	Outer rampart	68	Middle of face
	T2	94	Outer rampart	61	High on face
	T3	85	Low on face	0	None

FIGURE 87. PROBABILITY OF ATTACKER OR DEFENDER BEING HIT AT LEAST ONCE.

		Effectiveness					
Speed	Tactic	1	0.5	0.33	0.25	0.2	0.1	0.05
			Univallate					
Basic	T1	1	13	27	38	47	69	83
	T2	1	18	33	45	53	74	86
	T3	20	51	65	73	78	89	94
Fast	T1	1	14	29	41	49	71	84
	T2	2	20	37	48	56	76	87
	T3	27	59	72	79	83	91	96
Slow	T1	<1	7	19	30	38	67	79
	T2	1	17	33	44	53	73	86
	T3	14	44	59	68	74	86	93
			Bivallate					
Basic	T1	4	24	39	50	57	76	87
	T2	7	30	46	56	63	80	89
	T3	17	44	59	68	73	86	93
Fast	T1	8	30	46	56	63	80	89
	T2	12	39	54	63	70	84	91
	T3	28	56	69	76	80	90	95
Slow	T1	4	22	38	49	56	75	87
	T2	6	27	43	54	61	78	89
	T3	15	42	57	66	72	85	92

FIGURE 88. PROBABILITY OF ATTACKER REACHING HAND-TO-HAND DISTANCE.

Rampart	Effectiveness	Outcome	Outcome Favours?
		For reinforcements at 30 second intervals	
Uni	0.5	Rampart undefended for 20s after 2 rounds of slinging	Attack
	0.25	Rampart undefended for 10s after 4 rounds of slinging	Attack
	0.2	Rampart undefended for 5s after 5 rounds of slinging	Either
	0.17*	Rampart always defended (just)	Either
	0.1	Rampart always defended; defenders achieve numerical superiority after 12 rounds of slinging (about 1 minute)	Defence
Bi	0.05-1.0	Rampart always defended; defenders achieve numerical superiority after 12 rounds of slinging (1 minute)	Defence
		For Reinforcements at 15 second intervals	
Uni	0.5	Rampart undefended for 5s after 2 rounds of slinging. If not exploited, defence achieves numerical superiority after 9 rounds (45s)	Either
	0.05-0.33	Rampart always defended; defenders achieve numerical superiority after 9 rounds of slinging (45s)	Defence
Bi	0.05-1.0	Rampart always defended; defenders achieve numerical superiority after 6 rounds of slinging (30s)	Defence
		For Reinforcements at 60 second intervals	
Uni	0.5	Rampart undefended for 50s after 2 rounds of slinging	Attack
	0.13*	Rampart undefended for 20s after 8 rounds of slinging	Attack
	0.1	Rampart undefended for 5s after 11 rounds of slinging; if not exploited, defenders achieve numerical superiority after 36 rounds (3 minutes)	Either
	0.08*	Rampart always defended; defenders achieve numerical superiority after 24 rounds of slinging (2 minutes)	Defence
Bi	0.05-0.5	Rampart always defended; defenders achieve numerical superiority after 12 rounds of slinging (2 minutes)	Defence

*These values (hit effectiveness 1/6, 1/8 and 1/12) represent thresholds in the analysis.

FIGURE 89. EFFECT OF REINFORCING OUTNUMBERED DEFENDERS AT VARIOUS INTERVALS.

Bibliography

Alcock, L. 1972. *'By South Cadbury is that Camelot . .' Excavations at Cadbury Castle 1966-1970.* London, Thames and Hudson.

Andrushko, V. A. and Torres, E.C. 2011. Skeletal evidence for Inca warfare from the Cuzco region of Peru. *American Journal of Physical Anthropology* 146: 361-372.

Armit, I. 2007. Hillforts at war: from Maiden Castle to Taniwaha Pa. *Proceedings of the Prehistoric Society* 73: 25-38.

Avery, M. 1979. *Hill Fort Defences of Southern Britain: An Historical Study in Construction and Tactics.* Oxford, University of Oxford.

Avery, M. 1986. 'Stoning and fire' at hillfort entrances of southern Britain. *World Archaeology* 18: 216-230.

Avery, M. 1993a. *Hillfort Defences of Southern Britain: Vol. I, Ramparts, Entrances, Dating, Prehistory.* British Archaeological Reports British Series 231. Oxford, British Archaeological Reports.

Avery, M. 1993b. *Hillfort Defences of Southern Britain: Vol. II, The Evidence of Individual Sites.* British Archaeological Reports British Series 231. Oxford, British Archaeological Reports.

Avery, M. 1993c. *Hillfort Defences of Southern Britain: Vol. III, Appendices B to Y and Figures.* British Archaeological Reports British Series 231. Oxford, British Archaeological Reports.

Barrett, J. C., Freeman, P. W. M. and Woodward, A. 2000. *Cadbury Castle, Somerset.* London, English Heritage.

Bersu, G. 1940. Excavations at Little Woodbury, Wiltshire. Part 1: The settlement as revealed by excavation. *Proceedings of the Prehistoric Society* 6: 30-111.

Bishop, N. A. and Knüsel, C. J. 2005. A paleodemographic investigation of warfare in prehistory. In M. Parker Pearson and I. J. N. Thorp (eds.), *Warfare, Violence and Slavery in Prehistory.* British Archaeological Reports International Series 1374: 201-216. Oxford, Archaeopress.

Bowden, M. 1991. *Pitt Rivers: The Life and Archaeological Work of Lieutenant-General Augustus Henry Lane Fox Pitt Rivers, DCL, FRS, FSA.* Cambridge, Cambridge University Press.

Bowden, M. 2006. 'Guard chambers:' an unquestioned assumption in British Iron Age studies. *Proceedings of the Prehistoric Society* 72: 423-436.

Bowden, M. and Blood, N. K. 2004. Reassessment of two late prehistoric sites: Maiden Castle and Greenber Edge. In R. F. White and P. R. Wilson (eds.),

Archaeology and Historic Landscapes of the Yorkshire Dales. YAS Occasional Paper 2: 89-98. Leeds, Yorkshire Archaeological Society.

Bowden, M. and McOmish, D. 1987. The required barrier. *Scottish Archaeological Review* 4: 84-97.

Bowden, M. and McOmish, D. 1989. Little boxes: more about hillforts. *Scottish Archaeological Review* 6: 12-16.

Boyd Dawkins, W. 1900. The exploration of Hod Hill near Blandford, Dorset, in 1897. *Archaeological Journal* 57: 52-68.

Brown Vega, M. and Craig, N. 2009. New experimental data on the distance of sling projectiles. *Journal of Archaeological Science* 36: 1264-1268.

Brown, I. 2009. *Beacons in the Landscape: the Hillforts of England and Wales.* Oxford, Windgather Press.

Celsus (A. Cornelius Celsus). 1935. *De Medecina.* Vol. III of the Loeb Classical Library, Book VII: 4. http://penelope.uchicago.edu/Thayer/E/Roman/Texts/Celsus/7*.html (15 June 2013).

Cichorius, C. 1896. *Die Reliefs der Traianssäule, Erster Tafelband: Die Reliefs des Ersten Dakischen Krieges, Tafeln 1-57.* Berlin, Verlag von Georg Reimer.

Collis, J. R. 1975. *Defended Sites of the Late La Tene in Central and Western Europe.* British Archaeological Reports Supplementary Series 2. Oxford, British Archaeological Reports.

Collis, J. R. 1981. A theoretical study of hillforts. In G. Guilbert (ed.), *Hill-fort Studies: Essays for A. H. A. Hogg*: 66-76. Leicester, Leicester University Press.

Collis, J. R. 1984. *The European Iron Age.* London, Batsford.

Collis, J. R. 1996. Hill-forts, enclosures and boundaries. In T. C. Champion and J. R. Collis (eds.), *The Iron Age in Britain and Ireland*: *Recent Trends*: 87-94. Sheffield, Sheffield Academic Press.

Corney, M. 2006. The hillforts of Wessex: Their morphology and environs. In A. Payne, M. Corney and B. W. Cunliffe (eds.), *The Wessex Hillforts Project*: 131-150. London, English Heritage.

Craig, C. R., Knüsel, C. J. and Carr, G. C. 2005. Fragmentation, mutilation and dismemberment: An interpretation of human remains on Iron Age sites. In M. Parker Pearson and I. J. N. Thorpe (eds.), *Warfare, Violence and Slavery in Prehistory.* British Archaeological Reports International Series 1374: 165-180. Oxford, Archaeopress.

Cunliffe, B. W. 1984a. *Danebury, an Iron Age hillfort in Hampshire. Vol. 1, The Excavations 1969-1978: the Site.* London, Council for British Archaeology.

Cunliffe, B. W. 1984b. *Danebury, an Iron Age hillfort in Hampshire. Vol. 2, The Excavations 1969-1978: the Finds.* London, Council for British Archaeology.

Cunliffe, B. W. 1992. Pits, preconceptions and propitiation in the British Iron Age. *Oxford Journal of Archaeology* 11: 69-82.

Cunliffe, B. W. 1993. *Wessex to A.D. 1000.* Harlow, Adison Wesley Longman.

Cunliffe, B. W. 1995. *Danebury, an Iron Age hillfort in Hampshire. Vol. 6, A Hillfort Community in Perspective.* CBA Research Report 102. London, Council for British Archaeology.

Cunliffe, B. W. 2000. *The Danebury Environs Programme: The Prehistory of a Wessex Landscape. Vol. 1, Introduction.* Oxford, University of Oxford Committee for Archaeology.

Cunliffe, B. W. 2005. *Iron Age Communities in Britain.* 4th (paperback) edition. Abingdon, Routledge.

Cunliffe, B. W. 2006. Understanding hillforts: Have we progressed? In A. Payne, M. Corney and B. W. Cunliffe (eds.), *The Wessex Hillforts Project*: 151-162. London, English Heritage.

Cunliffe, B. W. and Poole, C. 1991. *Danebury, an Iron Age hillfort in Hampshire. Vol. 4, The Excavations 1978-1988: the Site.* CBA Research Report 73. London, Council for British Archaeology.

Cunnington, M. E. 1933. Excavations at Yarnbury Castle Camp, 1932. *Wiltshire Archaeological Magazine* 46: 198-213.

Darvill, T. 1987. *Prehistoric Britain.* London, B. T. Batsford.

Dawson, D. 1996. The origins of war: Biological and anthropological theories. *History and Theory* 35: 1-28.

Dawson, D. 1999. Evolutionary theory and group selection: The question of warfare. *History and Theory* 38: 79-100.

Dent, J. 1983. Weapons, wounds and war in the Iron Age. *Archaeological Journal* 140: 120-128.

Dixon, P. 1994. *Crickley Hill: Volume 1 - the Hillfort Defences.* Nottingham, University of Nottingham.

Dohrenwend, R. E. 2002. The sling: Forgotten firepower of antiquity. *Journal of Asian Martial Arts* 11: 28-49.

Dyer, J. 1981. *Hillforts of England and Wales.* Aylesbury, Shire.

Ellis, C. and Powell, A. B. 2008. *An Iron Age Settlement outside Battlesbury Hillfort, Warminster, and Sites along the Southern Range Road.* Salisbury, Wessex Archaeology.

Ellis, S. E. 1968. Notes on the stones from Hod Hill. In I. Richmond (ed.), *Hod Hill Volume Two: Excavations Carried Out between 1951 and 1958*: 135-137. London, Trustees of the British Museum.

Federacio Balear de Tir de Fona. 2012. *Reglaments.* www.tirdefona.org/catalan/marcocat.htm (26 March 2012).

Finney, J. B. 2006. *Middle Iron Age Warfare of the Hillfort Dominated Zone c. 400 BC to c. 150 BC.* British Archaeological Reports British Series 423. Oxford, British Archaeological Reports.

Fitzpatrick, A. P. and Morris E. L. 1994. Introduction: The changing Iron Age of Wessex. In A. P. Fitzpatrick and E. L. Morris (eds.), *The Iron Age in Wessex: Recent work*: x-xi. Salisbury, Association Francaise D'Etude de L'Age du Fer and Trust for Wessex Archaeology.

Fox, A. 1961. South-western hill-forts. In S. S. Frere (ed.), *Problems of the Iron Age in Southern Britain*: 35-60. London, University of London.

Fox, A., Quinnell, N. and Rouillard, M. 1987. *Milber Down.* DAS Field Guide Number One. Exeter, Devon Archaeological Society.

Glencross, E. and Boz, B. 2014. Representing violence in Anatolia and the Near East during the transition to agriculture: Readings from contextualized human skeletal remains. In C. Knüsel and M. J. Smith (eds.), *The Routledge Handbook of the Bioarchaeology of Human Conflict*: 90-108. Abingdon, Routledge.

Gosden, C. and Lock, G. 2007. The aesthetics of landscape on the Berkshire Downs. In C. Haselgrove and R. Pope (eds.), *The Earlier Iron Age in Britain and the Near Continent*: 279-292. Oxford, Oxbow Books.

Gray, C. D. and Kinnear, P. R. 2012. *IBM SPSS 19 Statistics Made Simple.* New York, Psychology Press.

Greep, S. J. 1987. Lead sling-shot from Windridge Farm, St. Albans and the use of the sling by the Roman Army in Britain. *Britannia* 18: 183-200.

Guilbert, G. 1975. Moel y Gaer, 1973: An area excavation on the defences. *Antiquity* 49: 109-117.

Gwilt, A. and Haselgrove, C. 1997. *Reconstructing Iron Age societies: New Approaches to the British Iron Age.* Oxford, Oxbow Books.

Hamilton, S. and Manley, J. 2001. Hillforts, monumentality and place: A chronological and topographic review of first millenium BC hillforts in southeast England. *Journal of European Archaeology* 4: 7-42.

Harbison, P. 1971. Wooden and stone *chevaux-de-frise* in western and central Europe. *Proceedings of the Prehistoric Society* 37: 195-225.

Harding, D. W. 1979. *Celts in Conflict: Hillfort Studies, 1927-77.* Edinburgh, University of Edinburgh.

Harding, D. W. 2004. *The Iron Age in Northern Britain.* Abingdon, Routledge.

Harding, D. W. 2012. *Iron Age Hillforts in Britain and Beyond.* Oxford, Oxford University Press.

Harrison, C. 2011. *Sling Ranges.* http://slinging.org/index.php?page=sling-ranges (1 July 2013).

Haselgrove, C. 2009. The Iron Age. In J. Hunter and I. Ralston (eds.), *The Archaeology of Britain - An Introduction from Earliest Times to the Twenty-first Century*: 149-174. Abingdon, Routledge.

Haselgrove, C., Armit, I., Champion, T., Creighton, J., Gwilt, A., Hill, J. D., Hunter, F. and Woodward, A. 2001. *Understanding the British Iron Age: An agenda for Action.* Salisbury, Trust for Wessex Archaeology.

Hawkes, C. F. C. 1931. Hill forts. *Antiquity* 5: 60-97.

Hawkins, W. 1847. Observations on the use of the sling as a warlike weapon among the ancients. *Archaeologia* XXXII: 92-107.

Heath, J. 2009. *Warfare in Prehistoric Britain.* Stroud, Amberley.

Heizer, R. F. and Johnson, I. W. 1952. A prehistoric sling from Lovelock Cave, Nevada. *American Antiquity* 18: 139-147.

Hencken, T. C. 1938. The excavation of the Iron Age camp on Bredon Hill, Gloucestershire, 1935-1937. *Archaeological Journal* 95: 1-111.

Hillfort Study Group. 2005. *Llyn Peninsula Field Guide, April 2005.* http://www.hillfortsstudygroup.org.uk/hfsgllyn2005.pdf (31 August 2013).

Hill, J. D. 1989. Re-thinking the Iron Age. *Scottish Archaeological Review* 6: 16-24.

Hill, J. D. 1993. Can we recognize a different European past? A contrasting archaeology of later prehistoric settlements in southern England. *Journal of European Archaeology* 1: 57-75.

Hill, J. D. 1995. How should we understand Iron Age societies and hillforts? A contextual study from southern Britain. In J. D. Hill and C. G. Cumberpatch (eds.), *Different Iron Ages - Studies on the Iron Age in Temperate Europe.* British Archaeological Report S602: 45-66. Oxford, Tempus Reparatum.

Hill, J. D. 1996. Hill-forts and the Iron Age of Wessex. In T. Champion and J. Collis (eds.), *The Iron Age in Britain and Ireland: Recent Trends*: 95-116. Sheffield, University of Sheffield.

Hill, P. and Wileman, J. 2002. *Landscapes of War: the Archaeology of Aggression and Defence.* Stroud, Tempus.

Hodder, I. 1986. *Reading the Past: Current Approaches to Interpretation in Archaeology.* Cambridge, Cambridge University Press.

Human Factors and Ergonomics Society. 2005. *HFES: Code of ethics.* http://www.hfes.org/web/AboutHFES/ethics.html (10 March 2012).

Institute for Archaeologists. 2010. *Bylaws: Code of conduct.* http://www.archaeologists.net/sites/default/files/node-files/code_conduct.pdf (10 March 2012).

James, S. 2007. A bloodless past: the pacification of Early Iron Age Britain. In C. Haselgrove and R. Pope (eds.), *The Earlier Iron Age in Britain and the Near Continent*: 160-173. Oxford, Oxbow Books.

Karl, R. 2008. Random coincidences or: the return of the Celtic to Iron Age Britain. *Proceedings of the Prehistoric Society* 74: 69-78.

Keeley, L. H. 1996. *War Before Civilization: the Myth of the Peaceful Savage.* Oxford, Oxford University Press.

Korfmann, M. 1973. The sling as a weapon. *Scientific American* 229: 34-42.

Lane Fox, A. H. 1869. An examination into the character and probable origin of the hill forts of Sussex. *Archaeologia* 42: 27-52.

Lane Fox, A. H. 1877. President's Address to the Anthropological Institute. *Journal of the Anthropological Institute* 6: 491-510.

Laws, K. 1991. The foreign stone. In N. M. Sharples (ed.), *Maiden Castle: Excavations and Field Survey, 1985-6.* EH Archaeological Report 19: 229-233. London, English Heritage.

Lock, G. 2007. Wessex hillforts after Danebury: Exporing boundaries. In C. Gosden, H. Hamerow, P. de Jersey and G. Lock (eds.), *Communities and Connections: Essays in Honour of Barry Cunliffe*: 341-356. Oxford, Oxford University Press.

Lock, G. 2011. Hillforts, emotional metaphors, and the Good Life: A response to Armit. *Proceedings of the Prehistoric Society* 77: 355–362.

Lock, G. and Gosden, C. 2002. *Hillforts of the Ridgeway.* http://www.arch.ox.ac.uk/HOR1.html (19 August 2013).

Lock, G., Gosden, C. and Daly, P. 2005. *Segsbury Camp: Excavations in 1996 and 1997 at an Iron Age Hillfort on the Oxfordshire Ridgeway.* Oxford, Oxford University School of Archaeology.

Lock, G., Miles, D., Palmer, S., and Cromarty, A. M. 2003. The hillfort. In D. Miles, S. Palmer, G. Lock, C. Gosden and A. M. Cromarty (eds.), *Uffington White Horse and its Landscape: Investigations at White Horse Hill, Uffington, 1989-95 and Tower Hill, Ashbury, 1993-4*: 61-78. Oxford, Oxford Archaeology.

Lock, G. and Ralston, I. 2012. The Hillforts Atlas Project. *South Somerset Archaeological Research Group 'Cadbury Day,' 5 October 2012.* South Somerset Archaeological Research Group, South Cadbury.

Lock, G. and Ralston, I. 2013. *Hillfort Atlas Project: The survey of Hillforts.* http://www.arch.ox.ac.uk/hillforts-atlas-survey.html (22 August 2013).

Mahr, H. 1964. Die Steinschleuder, einer der ältesten Waffen der Menscheit. *Waffen und Kostumkunde* 6: 118-129.

Manring, M. M., Hawk, A., Calhoun, J. H. and Andersen, R C. 2009. Treatment of war wounds: A historical review. *Clinical Orthopeadics and Related Research* 467: 2168-2191.

McOmish, D., Field, D. and Brown, G. 2002. *The Field Archaeology of the Salisbury Plan Training Area.* Swindon, English Heritage.

Mellersh, H. E. L. 1969. *Julius Caesar: The Gallic War and other Writings.* Geneva, Heron Books.

Miles, D., Palmer, S., Lock, G., Gosden, C. and Cromarty, A. M. 2003. *Uffington White Horse and its Landscape: Investigations at White Horse Hill, Uffington, 1989-95 and Tower Hill, Ashbury, 1993-4.* Oxford, Oxford Archaeology.

Morant, G. M. and Goodman, M. C. 1943. Note on the human remains from Maiden Castle. In R. E. M. Wheeler (ed.), *Maiden Castle, Dorset*: 356-360. Oxford, Research Report of the Committee of the Society of Antiquaries 12.

Mould, Q., Carlisle, I. and Cameron, E. 2003. *The Archaeology of York, Volume 17: The Small Finds. 16: Leather and Leatherworking in Anglo-Scandinavian and Medieval York.* York, Council for British Archaeology.

Mrowiec, H. S. and Gale, F. 2007. *Heather and Hillforts.* Ruthin, Royal Commision on the Ancient and Historical Monuments of Wales.

Mytum, H. 1999. Castell Henllys. *Current Archaeology* 161: 66-172.

Mytum, H. 2013. *Monumentality in Later Prehistory: Building and Rebuilding Castell Henllys Hillfort.* London, Springer.

O'Connor, B., Foster, J. and Saunders, C. 2000. Violence. In J. C. Barrett, P. W. M. Freeman and A. Woodward (eds.), *Cadbury Castle, Somerset: The Later Prehistoric and Early Historic Archaeology.* EH Archaeological Report 20: 235-242. London, English Heritage.

Palmer, R. 1984. *Danebury: An Iron Age hillfort in Hampshire. An aerial photographic interpretation of its environs.* London, RCHM(E).

Papworth, M. 2011. *The Search for the Durotriges: Dorset and the West Country in the Late Iron Age.* Stroud, The History Press.

Payne, A., Corney, M. and Cunliffe, B. W. 2006. *The Wessex Hillforts Project: Extensive Survey of Hillfort Interiors in Central Southern England.* London, English Heritage.

Pikoulis, E. A., Petropoulos, J. C., Tsigris, C., Pikoulis, N. K., Leppaniemi, A. E., Pavlakis, E., Gavrielatou, D., Burris, E., Bastounis, M. and Rich, N. 2004. Trauma management in ancient Greece: Value of surgical principles through the years. *World Journal of Surgery* 28: 425-430.

Poole, C. 1984. Objects of baked clay. In B. W. Cunliffe (ed.), *Danebury: An Iron Age hillfort in Hampshire. Vol. 2, The excavations, 1969-1978: The finds*: 398-407. London, Council for British Archaeology.

Poole, C. 1991. The small objects of daub and clay. In N. M. Sharples (ed.), *Maiden Castle: Excavations and field survey 1985-6*. EH Archaeological Report 19: 209-210. London, English Heritage.

Poole, C. 1995. Study 12: Pits and propitiation. In B. W. Cunliffe (ed.), *Danebury: an Iron Age hillfort in Hampshire. Vol. 6, A hillfort community in perspective.* CBA Research Report 102: 249-275. York, Council for British Archaeology.

Poole, C. 2000. Clay slingshot. In J. C. Barrett, P. W. M. Freeman and A. Woodward (eds.), *Cadbury Castle, Somerset: The Later Prehistoric and Early Historic Archaeology.* EH Archaeological Report 20: 247. London, English Heritage.

Ralston, I. 2006. *Celtic Fortifications.* Stroud, Tempus.

Redfern, R. C. 2009. Does cranial trauma provide evidence for projectile weaponry in Late Iron Age Dorset? *Oxford Journal of Archaeology* 28: 399-424.

Richardson, T. 1998. The ballistics of the sling. Royal Armouries Yearbook 3: 44. http://slinging.org/index.php?page=the-ballistics-of-the-sling---thom-richardson (1 March 2013).

Richmond, I. 1968. *Hod Hill. Volume two, Excavations Carried Out between 1951 and 1958 for the Trustees of the British Museum.* London, Trustees of the British Museum.

Rivet, A. L. F. 1971. Hill-forts in action. In D. Hill and M. Jesson (eds.), *The Iron Age and its Hill-forts: Papers Presented to Sir Mortimer Wheeler on the Occasion of His Eightieth Year*: 189-202. Southampton, University of Southampton Archaeological Society.

Roe, F. 2005. The worked stone. In G. Lock, C. Gosden and P. Daly (eds.), *Segsbury Camp: Excavations in 1996 and 1997 at an Iron Age Hillfort on the Oxfordshire Ridgeway*: 122-123. Oxford, Oxford University School of Archaeology.

Seanchaidh. 2012. Cúchulain the champion of Ireland. http://seanchaidh.tripod.com/cuchulain.htm (27 March 2012).

Selwood, L. 1984. Objects of iron. In B. W. Cunliffe (ed.), *Danebury, an Iron Age hillfort in Hampshire. Vol. 2, The excavations 1969-1978: the finds*: 346-371. London, Council for British Archaeology.

Shanks, M. and Tilley, C. 1987. *Social Theory and Archaeology.* Oxford, Polity Press.

Sharples, N. M. 1991a. Warfare in the Iron Age of Wessex. *Scottish Archaeological Review* 8: 79-89.

Sharples, N. M. 1991b. *Maiden Castle: Excavations and Field Survey, 1985-6.* EH Archaeological Report 19. London, English Heritage.

Sharples, N. M. 1994. Maiden Castle, Dorset. In A. P. Fitpatrick and E. L. Morris (eds.), *The Iron Age in Wessex: Recent Work*: 91-93. Salisbury, Association Francaise D'Etude de L'Age du Fer and Trust for Wessex Archaeology.

Sharples, N. M. 2010. *Social Relations in Later Prehistory: Wessex in the First Millennium BC.* Oxford, Oxford University Press.

Skov, E. T. 2013. *Experimentation in Sling Weaponry: Effectiveness of and Archaeological Implications for a World-wide Primitive Technology.* Anthropology Department Dissertation, Paper 30. Lincoln, Nebraska, University of Nebraska.

Stanford, S. C. 1984. The Wrekin hillfort: Excavations 1973. *Archaeological Journal* 141: 61-90.

Stanford, S. C. and Greig, J. R. A. 1974. *Croft Ambrey: Excavations Carried Out for the Woolhope Naturalists' Field Club (Herefordshire) 1960-1966.* Hereford, Woolhope Naturalists' Field Club.

Stead, I. 1991. Many more Iron Age shields from Britain. *Antiquaries Journal* 71: 1-35.

Stead, I. M. 1998. *The Salisbury Hoard.* London, Tempus.

Stewart, D. A. 2006. *Assessing the Condition of Archaeological Remains: A Multi-method Geophysical Study at Hod Hill, Dorset.* Unpublished Dissertation, University of Bournemouth.

Stewart, D. A. 2008. Hod Hill: 'Too much wasted by cultivation for definite survey.' *Proceedings of the Dorset Natural History and Archaeology Society* 129: 97-103.

Tabor, R. 2008. *Cadbury Castle: The Hillfort and Landscapes.* Stroud, The History Press.

Tabor, R. 2012. The South Cadbury Environs Project. *South Somerset Archaeological Research Group 'Cadbury Day,' 5 October 2012.* South Somerset Archaeological Research Group, South Cadbury.

Thorpe, I. J. N. 2005. The ancient origins of warfare and violence. In M. Parker Pearson and I. J. N. Thorpe (eds.), *Warfare, Violence and Slavery in Prehistory.* British Archaeological Reports International Series 1374: 1-18. Oxford, Archaeopress.

Timberlake, S. 2013. Worked, utilised and burnt stone. In M. Brittain (ed.), *Excavations at Ham Hill, Somerset (2012)*: 71-81. Cambridge, Cambridge Archaeological Unit.

USHA/UCEA. 2011. *Guidance on Health and Safety in Fieldwork.* Eastbourne and London, Universities Safety and Health Association and Universities and Colleges Employers Association.

van Broekhoven, W. 2012. The underestimated weapon: The evolution of the humble sling. *Ancient Warfare* VI-4: 42-45.

Vegetius (Flavius Vegetius Renatus). 1767. The Military Institutions of the Romans *(De Re Militari)*. Translated from the Latin by Lt John Clarke, 1767. http://www.digitalattic.org/home/war/vegetius/ (10 June 2013).

Waddington, C. 2011a. *Fin Cop Excavation Archive Report for 2010.* ARS Report 2011/27. Bakewell, Archaeological Research Services Ltd.

Waddington, C. 2011b. Massacre at Fin Cop: new evidence of an Iron Age hillfort at war. *Current Archaeology* Issue 255: 20-27.

Wainwright, G. J. and Davies, S. M. 1995. *Balksbury Camp, Hampshire: Excavations 1973 and 1981.* EH Archaeological Report 4. London, English Heritage.

Weir, A. 2013. Stone forts, souterains and crannogs: Ending prehistory. http://www.irishmegaliths.org.uk/zDunAengusCdF.htm (6 September 2013).

Wheeler, R. E. M. 1943. *Maiden Castle, Dorset.* Oxford, Research Report of the Committee of the Society of Antiquaries 12.

York, R. and York, G. 2011. *Slings and Slingstones: The Forgotten Weapons of Oceania and the Americas.* Kent, Ohio, Kent State University Press.

Young, A. and Richardson, K. M. 1954-5. Report on the Excavations at Blackbury Camp. *Proceedings of the Devon Archaeological Exploration Society* 2 & 3: 43-67.